53-55 EDWIN ST. DORCHESTER, MA.   S. SWEETSER

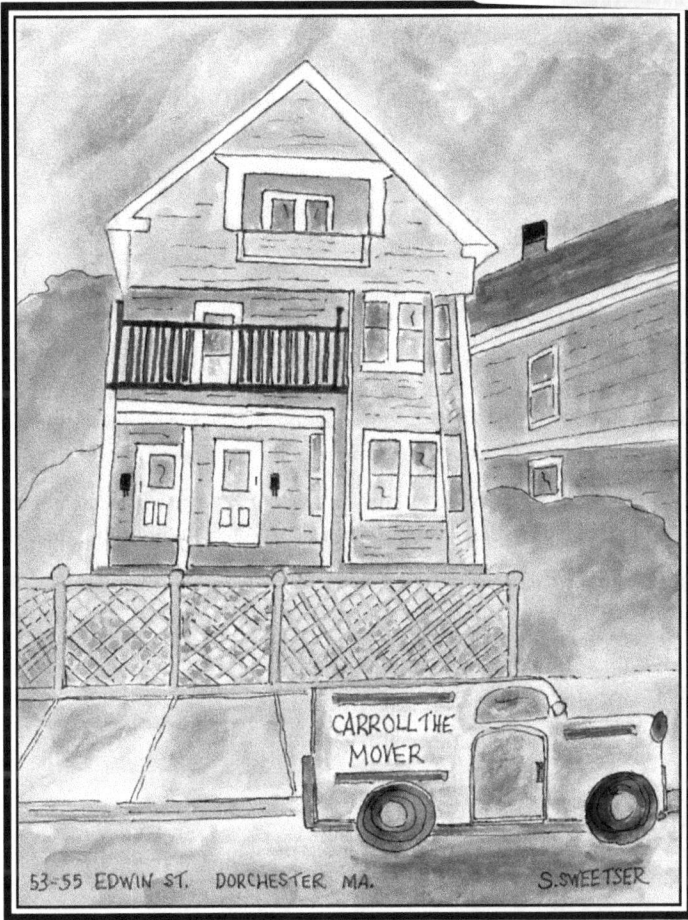

Since Dorchester

By
JUDITH KIRWAN KELLEY

Since Dorchester, published June, 2023
Editorial and proofreading services: Beth Raps and Kent Sorsky
Interior layout and cover design: Howard Johnson
Photo credits: front cover: Sandra Sweetser Watercolors, Duxbury, MA

SDP Publishing

Published by SDP Publishing, an imprint of SDP Publishing Solutions, LLC.

The stories in this book reflect the author's recollection of events. Some names, locations, and identifying characteristics have been changed to protect the privacy of those depicted.

To obtain permission(s) to use material from this work, please submit an email request with subject line "SDP Publishing Permissions Department" to info@SDPPublishing.com.

ISBN-13 (print): 979-8-9862833-8-8
ISBN-13 (ebook): 979-8-9862833-9-5

Library of Congress Control Number: 2023908846

Dedication

Since Dorchester is dedicated with all of my love to my family. You are my heart for life: my beloved husband Richard J. Kelley, Jr.; my daughters and their families: Kara Kelley Katz and Max Katz; Lindsey and Vasudev Mandyam, and Malini, Raja, and Nayan Mandyam; Courtney and Ryan Viveiros, and Grace and Hannah Viveiros.

Acknowledgments

I want to gratefully acknowledge both my publisher, Lisa Akoury-Ross, and my editor, Beth Raps. They responded consistently and kindly with encouragement and humor and convinced me that I once again had a legitimate, authoritative, and genuine set of stories to tell. Both Lisa and Beth completed extensive work on the drafts of both my current book, *Since Dorchester*, and my first book, *Dorchester Girl*.

Lisa and Beth also prompted me to take the time I needed when life interfered with my work, and together ushered me through the completion of this project.

I also want to acknowledge the role played by Kennedy Center Honors award-winning singer and songwriter Carole King's personal story as portrayed in the Broadway musical *Beautiful* in my quest to write and publish my written work.

I considered myself to be a writer since the age of eight, although my work was in the "scraps of notes" stage rather than the formal writing stage for decades of my life. The original production of *Beautiful* opened on Broadway in 2014, and I was fortunate to see it with my husband soon afterward. I was absolutely awed by the portrayal of 16-year-old Brooklyn girl Carole, who, in 1958, had the talent, the confidence, and the savvy to insist to her reluctant mother that she was going to go into Manhattan. Carole's objective was to find a music publisher and sell her work. As mothers are wont to do, her mother refused to let her go, and insisted that Carole must be at least 18 to pursue this plan. Carole enlisted the aid of an 18-year-old friend to accompany her into New York City, and did, in fact, sing and sell her composition "It Might as Well Rain Until September" to music publisher Donnie Kirshner. Kirshner recognized her stellar talent and asked her immediately if she had more songs that he could buy from her. Carole King's immensely successful career was thus launched.

I sat in the audience watching open-mouthed as these scenes of the teenaged Carole King played out. I asked myself repeatedly, "Where is my courage? What is holding me back from writing, rather than just talking so much about my goal of publishing at least one book about my own stories of my upbringing in a large Irish Catholic family in the Dorchester neighborhood of Boston, Massachusetts?"

At the conclusion of *Beautiful* that fateful day, I left Broadway determined that my notes would pile up no longer. I commenced compiling both formal and informal genealogical, historical, social, and family history notes, and finally wrote my first published book, *Dorchester Girl*. It is with continued gratitude for the influence of my family, Lisa Akoury-Ross, Beth Raps, and singer-songwriter Carole King that I now present my second book, *Since Dorchester*.

You own everything that happened to you. Tell your stories.

If people wanted you to write warmly about them, they should have treated you better.

—Anne Lamott

Table of Contents

1

⌒∾⌒

Beyond Civilization as I Knew It: First Impressions of Weymouth, Massachusetts

In my family, my hardworking Irish-American father demanded that there always be a semblance of order, as least as much as there could be with an ever-enlarging family and frequent changes in housing and school statuses. One inviolable rule was that suppertime be an event where the evening meal was prepared by my mother and on the table at exactly 4:15 p.m. on weekdays. The second rule was that all children be clean, quiet, and seated without any elbows on the table. Official mealtime did not commence until my father was in his place at the head of the table and took his first bite. After that, the rest of us could dig in.

Mealtime needed to be systematized, and it was. The three oldest girls would help my mother prepare and serve the meal, but my mother never sat for her supper until the older girls took their respective places beside each of the youngest (still in high chairs) to assist in their feeding. Likewise, supper did not end until my father declared that it had ended. The end of supper was routinely interrupted if he saw that any one of us had not finished every bite of food on our plates. If there were any parts of the dinner remaining, the eater would be reminded of a simple fact intended to restore the flagging appetite: for instance, my father would demand, "Do you have any idea how many hours I worked to purchase that bit of ground beef that is still on your plate?" Or he would remind us about all the starving children throughout the world whose lives would be enriched by the mere availability of what we were so callously planning to scrape into the garbage pail.

After the mealtime routine had concluded, each of us had to ask in turn, "May I please be excused?" My father would then dole out the tasks that must commence immediately post-dinner. (I always grabbed the youngest kids to bathe and get ready for bed, as I hated to do the dishes). Only then would we be allowed to go and complete our homework.

On one unusual evening, my mother quickly got up after we had all finished dinner and hurriedly cleared off the table herself. She grabbed us girls to wash, dry, and put away the dishes, and instructed all of us that we must be assembled at the freshly cleaned table in fifteen minutes exactly. The youngest kids were to be held quietly on the laps of the oldest before the intended lecture commenced. We all knew better than to defy my father's wishes. Kathy, Jeanie, Lonnie, and I did as bidden and took our seats again at the kitchen table. Once there, we quickly noticed an abundance of unfamiliar literature arrayed before us. My father had on his "lecture" countenance, while my mother stood by his side to support whatever he had to announce.

My father never spoke without a lengthy preamble. This time he was informing us older four kids about all the benefits of South Weymouth, Massachusetts. As always, I resisted the temptation to defy my father and say, "Who cares about Weymouth?" My incentive to keep my mouth shut was that I realized that I would not be able to eat the dessert that was waiting on the counter if I had a fat lip from a wise-ass response to my father.

So, we four older ones instead looked curiously at the literature spread about the table regarding Weymouth's statistics, trends, amenities, and quality of public school education, including the percentage of students graduating from Weymouth High School who attended four-year colleges.

My parents both talked (that is, my father lectured as my mother gently tried to sell us on Weymouth). We finally all realized it. This was not a "What would you think about the idea of moving from Dorchester to Weymouth?" inquiry, but a rather inept yet ultimately effective way of telling us that we were soon to move out of my beloved Dorchester. No questions or comments to the contrary would be tolerated.

What was pertinent to this major life event, the moving of the family, was that this was a very commonplace event, particularly for city dwellers during the baby boom years (1946–1964). Essentially, young couples married, got a small apartment, and moved into a slightly larger but still affordable apartment when they began having children. Particularly with Irish-American families, which tended to be larger, moving more often was a necessity rather than a luxury. My father was from a family of ten (eleven children were born to my grandparents, but one died at birth). Among my father and his nine surviving siblings alone, the average number of children per family was seven. Of ten surviving children born to my Kirwan grandparents, four went on to produce seven (or more) children each. As the number of children in each Irish-American family increased, it was often necessary for the family to move to relatively larger living quarters to accommodate all the kids. Moving was a fact of life, and not an anomaly for me and my siblings and cousins.

My father loved to tease (often) and tell me (often) that they moved (so often) that I would come home from school some day and find that they were all gone. I had nightmares about this (often).

For this and other reasons, suburban migration was taking place for the Kirwan family. It had already been determined that our next move would be to South Weymouth on the South Shore of Boston. In fact, my father's long-time employer, Codman and Shurtleff, was likewise leaving Savin Hill in Dorchester. Having been taken over by a leading US medical products manufacturer and distributor, the company was renamed Codman and relocated to its own large facility in Randolph, Massachusetts. (As Codman's new Randolph facility was just a slightly longer commute from Dorchester than it was to the long-time Savin Hill location of his employer, I was suspicious of my father's justification that we had to leave Dorchester since he'd be working "all the way in Randolph." However, he was fully aware that I was a hard sell on moving out of Dorchester, and he would use whatever justifications he had at hand to limit my expected objections to the move.)

I was absolutely stunned. I hadn't anticipated a move when we were called back to the table for this sudden presentation of demographic data. Moving in and of itself was not the issue. Moving out of Dorchester had me flummoxed and frustrated. The descriptive data that my parents were presenting to us about Weymouth did nothing to assuage my breaking heart.

In the absence of a slide show, my father continued his slow-paced didactic lecture (e.g., Weymouth was the second-oldest town in Massachusetts; early settlers sailed up Weymouth River to establish Wessagusset Colony; the town was the birthplace of Abigail Adams, who was the wife of President John Adams and mother of President John Quincy Adams; *we would be living not far from the site of Stetson Shoe Factory . . .*).

Oops! My father had slipped. He had just given us not mere objective information but *subjective* information: we *would* be living in Weymouth!

Realizing that he had precipitously shown his hand, both parents hastened to fill in what they had neglected to inform us of at the beginning of tonight's lecture: they had already purchased a four-bedroom Cape-Cod-style home with an attached garage and a large yard with a white picket fence in a residential neighborhood. We would soon be moving from Dorchester to a home on Bald Eagle Road in South Weymouth.

My very first thought was, "*Girls' Latin, Girls' Latin!* How can I commute from South Weymouth to Girls' Latin?" I had struggled so much through seventh grade, having failed two classes and having had to spend the intervening summer in remedial classes in order to be readmitted to the most challenging and beloved educational institution of my life so far!

Admittedly, I had hated my first year of Boston's Girls' Latin High School, especially when I learned that I would have to attend summer school in order to return after failing two courses in grade seven. It was a hard-won victory, and I learned *how* to learn in summer school at Boston (Boys') Latin. I went back to eighth grade, earning As and Bs in all my classes. I looked forward to the day when my sister and I would graduate from the prestigious institution, which was the first public high school in America, founded in 1635. Boston Girls' Latin School was founded in 1878. Eventually the school became co-ed, but in my time, co-educational learning at Boys' Latin School was for summer school only.

At this point, then, I was academically skilled, had many friends who lived throughout the city of Boston, loved the atmosphere of the dilapidated, yellow-brick school building in Codman Square, and was determined that I was *not* going to leave Dorchester again!

All the other kids in my family seemed to take it in stride that as one body, we would simply pick up and move. And this was our third time in four years. But not me! I was devastated! I begged my parents to let me stay in the apartment on Edwin Street in Dorchester where we were living. I was used to taking care of other people, so I could certainly take care of just myself. I knew how to clean and cook, and I would be at Girls' Latin five days a week anyway. My grandmother, aunt, and a cousin lived right in Codman Square. I could go to them if I needed anything. I earned a good amount of money by babysitting for neighbors and cousins, cleaning house for my aunt, and making and selling woven potholders.

My mother and father laughed, my father not as hard as my mother did. His face was more grim than amused. I was being recalcitrant, as usual. Actually, he said I was an "obstinate obstacle." He was not happy with me. My mother thought she could take the wind out of my sails.

"How would you pay the rent?" she challenged. I had a ready answer for her. In a rare moment of sharing a confidence with me, my mother had told me that, with all the upgrades to the Edwin Street apartments that she and my father had made over the years since they first purchased the house, the rents that they took in paid all but seven dollars of the mortgage. My quick response was that I easily earn more than seven dollars a month! I could pay it and then I could stay here!

My father's temper was exhausted. He shouted at me, "Shut up and get packing. And pack the little kids' things as well!"

I had lost the battle. Within weeks we would be gone and living in a town called South Weymouth. I thought, "South Nowhere! It is not Dorchester. It isn't even anywhere in Boston!"

Despite my strenuous objections to leaving Dorchester, my parents sold the house out from under me. I clearly remember the threat from my father to place me in the moving truck along with the furniture if I didn't come along peaceably on the day we were scheduled to move to South Weymouth.

The family was unable to complete the entire move to South Weymouth in time for the 1968–1969 school year to begin. I had fervently hoped that this would allow for a transition year at Girls' Latin for Kathy and me before we became part of the Weymouth school system. But that was not to be. Even though we were all physically living in the Edwin Street house, the four older Kirwan kids began the 1968–1969 school year in South Weymouth.

For the first few weeks, we commuted to school from Dorchester, with my father delivering us to our respective school buildings in South Weymouth. He would leave work early and be there at the end of the day to drive us home to Dorchester. I made it a habit for the last bit of time in Dorchester to race from Edwin Street to Talbot Avenue to see as many of my former teachers and friends as I could. (They got out of Girls' Latin School later in the afternoon than we did from the Weymouth schools.) It was a (very mixed) blessing to be able to see them all again, but it broke my heart that I was no longer a Girls' Latin School student.

I was soon enrolled at and attending classes at South Junior High School in Weymouth, but home remained Edwin Street in Dorchester for a few weeks until we officially moved. There, I'd sit on the front porch with my long-time best friend Joanie, and I would tell her bits and pieces about the students who attended South Junior High. I felt like a girl who had no place to call home, or even my own school. It became very difficult to put on a brave face about moving when all I really wanted was to stay in Dorchester. However, I started to grudgingly acknowledge to myself that it was becoming painful to be caught between two lives: the Dorchester life and the about-to-begin South Weymouth life. I resided mere weeks later in South Weymouth, attending the Weymouth school system through high school graduation in 1972.

Since the die was cast when my father had inadvertently acknowledged that we *would* soon be living in Weymouth, I had quietly sequestered the literature about our new town that my parents had spread around the kitchen table. I reverted to my younger years' habit of hiding under my bed to read. As a child, I hid to keep my mother from sending me outdoors to play when I would rather be reading. This time, I hid under my bed to read the relevant literature only because I did not want my parents to catch on that I was coming around to the idea of actually moving to

Weymouth. I grudgingly accepted the inevitable and wanted to be prepared for my new surroundings. My gloomy assumption was that, unlike Boston, there would be nothing to do. There would be no excitement, no place to go, just a boring suburb in which to while our time away until I moved out on my own.

What I learned from my surreptitious research was that Weymouth, Massachusetts, is a city in Norfolk County, yet is one of 13 municipalities in the state to retain "town" in their official names. The city is named after Weymouth, Dorset, in England, and is the second-oldest settlement in Massachusetts after Plymouth. Weymouth is a short commute into Boston. Wessagusset Beach in North Weymouth is the city's beach.

Wessagusset was established in 1623. Early settlers wanted a form of government more equal than that which they had left behind in England. By 1635 the population rose to more than 300 people. The name of the town was changed to Weymouth and was recognized as part of the Massachusetts Bay Colony. Weymouth established the first town meeting in 1641. For 200 years, what became the city of Weymouth was known as a fishing and agricultural community.

After the Industrial Revolution, Weymouth became a manufacturing town. By 1880, the shoe industry was the most important, with close to 75 shoe factories employing one-third of the population. Weymouth's main shoe factory, the Stetson Shoe Company, opened in 1885 and only closed its doors in 1973.

The city's second-largest employer was Weymouth Iron Works, which operated from 1837 to 1890, employing 300 residents. Granite quarries in Weymouth employed close to 300 as well.

The South Weymouth Naval Air Station was an operational US Navy airfield from 1942 to 1997. During the postwar era, its primary function was as a training facility. The base was also constructed to provide housing and be the center of life for thousands of servicemen (and later servicewomen) all over the country.

During the postwar era, the base became part of the Naval Air Parking Station.

This last bit of information to me at the time seemed completely irrelevant. What would *my* family ever have to do with the South Weymouth Naval Air Station? I found out a few years later.

In the years during which we lived in Weymouth, we would go as a family to the naval air shows held on the base to watch performances by members of the US Navy's and Marine Corps' Aerial Aerobatic Demonstration Teams. The air base was overrun with thousands of visitors from Weymouth and far beyond who came for the thrill of being part of this event.

On September 8, 1974, the Navy's Blue Angels performed for the public at the popular air show. At age 20 and no longer living at home, I attended the naval air show on this date with my parents and younger siblings. People of all ages, from toddlers to the elderly, eagerly anticipated the air show events.

Especially eagerly anticipated was an event in which one young female pilot was scheduled to perform a solo maneuver. Tragically, during the stunt, her Bellanca 8KCAB crashed nearly vertically into the ground while performing a controlled acrobatic half-twist. It ignited upon impact. The cause of the crash was that the pilot had misjudged her altitude and clearance. She was killed in the crash. Equally tragic was that her husband was also a Blue Angels pilot who was watching his wife's performance as her plane dove into the airfield.

What was as stunning to me as the crash itself was how well crowd control was maintained by the military organizers. When the small plane rose to the sky, most eyes were on it. Suddenly all was quiet as the plane came plummeting to the ground. All that was visible to the crowd was smoke. There was no outcry, no screaming from the crowd, no emergency declarations from staff. Among the audience were hundreds of children. I kept looking back and forth at other members of the huge crowd to see if anyone else had seen what I had just witnessed. It was eerily quiet, with absolute control of the audience maintained by the naval air station staff. A large wooden fence separated the airfield from the onlookers, and the debris field was well apart from the show attendees.

I couldn't believe what I had seen. I started to run toward the barrier fence, and my father grabbed my shoulder to stop me. I shook off his hand roughly, without even thinking, and ran toward the wreckage of what had been the small plane. Few others did the same. As I got to the fence, I stared in disbelief at the smoking mound of metal. What flabbergasted me was that no emergencies were announced, no sirens sounded. A sole ambulance drove silently to the site of the crash. To this day, I honor the crisis teams for maintaining such a total degree of calm, thanks to the emergency response plans they had in place.

Operationally, the naval air station in South Weymouth remained a United States Navy airfield until 1997. In 1986, while assessing possible uses for the soon-to-close air station, the Base Realignment and Closure Commission detected significant levels of environmental contamination. Since 1993, numerous remedies and long-term monitoring of groundwater have been in place.

In March 1998, the Massachusetts legislature established the South Shore Tri-Town Development Corporation, representing Abington, Rockland, and Weymouth, the three towns that had been a part of the naval air station.

After the shoe industry and the South Weymouth Naval Air Station waned as significant sources of employment, Weymouth became a bedroom community for those working in Boston and other cities and towns in the area.

Weymouth est omnis divisa in partes quattuor. (What would you expect from a Latin School girl?) The translation of my descriptive phrase is that "All Weymouth is divided into four parts." These are North Weymouth, South Weymouth, East Weymouth, and Weymouth Landing.

North Weymouth includes anything north of Church Street, North Street, and Green Street. It is the most densely populated area. Some of the sites around North Weymouth are Great Esker Park, George Lane Beach, Webb State Park, the Wessagussett Yacht Club, skyline views of Boston, and the Abigail Adams Historical Society. Personally, I would have opted for the skyline views of Boston since I couldn't be in Boston proper.

South Weymouth is mostly south of Route 3 and home to the former naval air station. This part of the town has since been redeveloped into residential and commercial properties and has one of the area's biggest housing developments. The single-family homes were plentiful, affordable, and had generous floor plans. Outside, the front and back yards accommodated gardens and areas for family leisure. A significant number of houses also had garages and private driveways. For those of us who had always had to search for parking in Boston (even in front of our own homes, at times), the driveways and garages attached to most suburban homes might have been the biggest draw to suburban living.

East Weymouth is considered to be the center of Weymouth. Whitman's Pond, Jackson Square, and the Weymouth Town Hall are located in East Weymouth. Weymouth Landing spans a mile around Weston Park. The commercial areas of Weymouth Landing have been under redevelopment since the 1970s. Weymouth Landing is the border between Weymouth and Braintree, and where the Fore River splits into tributaries.

South Shore Hospital and Weymouth High School are located in South Weymouth, as is its own town center, Columbian Square. At the time of our intended move in 1968, Weymouth was in the process of building new schools. Weymouth High School on Commercial Street in East Weymouth would become known as Weymouth North High when Weymouth South High School opened (on Pleasant Street in South Weymouth) for its incoming class in September 1970. The first class to graduate from Weymouth South High School was the class of 1971. The schools for elementary-aged children through high school kids were within walking distance or a relatively short school bus ride. Our new Catholic church (Saint Francis Xavier Church) was less than half a mile away. Part-time work opportunities for the teenage children were readily available. My parents made sure that Kathy and I, and then Jeanie, were quickly employed as soon as we could obtain our working papers. For me, that was at age 14. Considering all factors, South Weymouth was our family's choice.

2

⚜

Why the Kirwan Family Moved Out of Dorchester in 1968

A particularly pertinent question to be answered is *"Why* did the Kirwan family move out of Dorchester in 1968?"

The short answer in terms of my family was upward social mobility. The term "social mobility" refers to the movements of individuals, families, households, or other categories of people between social classes in a society. It is most often a change to one's social status relative to one's current social location in a society. At least some value is given to achieved status characteristics in a society, especially relative to upward mobility. Worth noting is the fact that achieved status characteristics such as education and social class have a significant impact on social mobility.

As my parents both attended Northeastern University at night, it became increasingly difficult for my mother to keep up with family, additional children, housework, and homework. I am not sure what her preference would have been, had she been asked, but she gave up her college classes to focus on the family. My father continued to attend Northeastern until he graduated with a bachelor's degree in mechanical engineering when I was ten years old.

In terms of social class, my father was no longer designated as a laborer once he had earned his bachelor's. After he had completed his student teaching requirement and had been offered a job in a suburban school system, my father was set to change careers, but not necessarily his income level. However, his employers at Codman realized that they were allowing to leave an employee with over 15 years of hands-on surgical instrument manufacturing and repair experience, and now a bachelor's degree in mechanical engineering. Codman offered him a significant promotion and a substantial increase in salary to stay—now at the executive level in the company. My father accepted, and with the changes he was now a "suit" and a family man with an income that allowed for desired life improvements to take place.

So, from Dorchester, we moved with our family of then six children to South Weymouth, Massachusetts, a mere 20 minutes away via routes I-93 South and MA-3 South. It was a whole new world.

It was strange, and new, and welcome that we were in a single-family home in the suburbs rather than in an urban metropolitan area. The house lots in South Weymouth were significantly larger than the narrow tracts on which the triple-deckers had been built in Dorchester.

Many of the homes in our new neighborhood had attached garages, so there was very little reason to park in the roads. We were not limited to playing Red Rover, and softball, and other games in busy streets as we had most of our lives since here there were generous backyards. I noticed immediately that there were hardly any curbs in the neighborhoods. It seems odd that an almost-14-year-old would miss curbs, but in my young childhood, playing outside unattended, they had defined the limits of unsupervised play space. For instance, my mother might say, "You can walk down Parkman Street but do not go past the curb to cross Dorchester Avenue." Curbs were significant to me, and I noticed that there were few curbs in the suburban neighborhoods in South Weymouth.

The omnipresent drainage gutters in Dorchester were absent in most of the residential neighborhoods in Weymouth. Grassy yards were demarcated by privately owned fences. The front yards and driveways simply tapered off to the residential streets. How could we play baseball in the street if we didn't have gutters and sewers for boundaries and bases? How could we play hide-and-go-seek if there weren't as many telephone poles on which to hide our faces till everybody hid? How could everybody crouch down behind and between parked cars if they were all in private driveways or parked inside garages?

I sincerely missed my Dorchester homes, friends, and relatives. One consolation was that "white flight" (the exodus or large-scale migration of white people from areas becoming more racially or ethnoculturally diverse) had resulted in many people who were originally from Dorchester (OFD) living, working, and going to school in Weymouth. And one other bonus that I discovered rather quickly was that a bus from Columbian Square would take me to South Shore Plaza in Braintree, where I could get a bus to Ashmont in Dorchester. Once I was at Ashmont, I had access to the Red Line trains. I could go back to Dorchester as often as I wanted, and I did. I had easy access via train to "in town," also known as "downtown," then later as "Downtown Crossing."

The hardest obstacle that I had to overcome shortly after moving to South Weymouth was how very much I missed my school friends, the teachers, and the culture of Girls' Latin School. As I write this book at age 67, I have on my windowsill, within reach of my desk, a wooden representation of the very same Boston Girls' Latin School. This was given to me a number of years ago by my sister Kathy, who is the only one who could possibly understand what leaving Latin meant to both of us.

3

⤫

Gobsmacked! The Earlier Move Out of Dorchester

During my early Dorchester childhood, my family lived in rented apartments in multifamily houses on Faulkner Street in Fields Corner, and on Parkman Street. My parents became first-time homeowners with the purchase of the two-and-a-half-story house, which was numbered both 53 and 55 Edwin St.

Wherever I lived in Dorchester, I was blissfully happy. However, when I was 12, we moved to a brand-new garrison colonial home on Franclaire Drive in the long-established leafy suburb of West Roxbury. West Roxbury was within the boundaries of the city of Boston, but it was nestled in the southwest corner. Often mistakenly confused with Roxbury, the two parts of the city of Boston are separated by six miles. We lived adjacent to Roslindale, which is northeast of West Roxbury, and also part of the city of Boston. The city of Newton lies directly northwest and the town of Dedham southwest of West Roxbury.

As much as I was in love with my status as a resident of Dorchester, I was pleasantly surprised to fall in love with our home and neighborhood in West Roxbury.

My sister Kathy and I, then students in our second year at Girls' Latin School, commuted by public transportation each day while my father drove Jeanie and Lonnie to their respective schools, which were still in Dorchester.

We all absolutely adored our first brand-new home, made more special to us by the fact that it was a single-family dwelling. We had no neighbors upstairs or downstairs; all the commotion in the house was our own! As impressive was the fact that we had two bathrooms. For our big family in Dorchester, we had always had just one bathroom for the whole family to share. This was the most vexing inconvenience about our living accommodations. Having two bathrooms for our big family was like living in a palace. On seeing an empty bathroom in our West Roxbury home, one or the other of the kids would decide to make use of it, just because we could! No more of all of the kids doing the pee-pee dance outside the sole bathroom as my father took his time getting ready for work.

While in West Roxbury, Saint Theresa's was our family's parish. But geographically, it was quicker for us, as kids, to cut through the multiple construction sites in our neighborhood to attend Saint John Chrysostom Church, closer to Roslindale.

Jeanie and I, in particular, were madly in love with our new home, and did all that we could to enhance our family's enjoyment of it. Although we were more typically "outside" kids, we spent a great deal of our free time enjoying the inside of our new home. Together on Sundays, Jeanie and I climbed hills and valleys through the building sites, attended early morning Mass, and scurried home the same way. My parents availed themselves of the opportunity to go to late Mass.

The youngest in the family at the time, three-year-old Christine, became my responsibility—quite amenably both to Christine and to me! Jeanie scoured clean the living room and dining room and made the beds. I fed, changed, and entertained my little sister until it was time for Jeanie and me to make Sunday dinner. We sang while we peeled potatoes and prepared the rest of the meal. In Dorchester, it had taken a lot of prodding on my mother's part to get us to do any of these chores. But in West Roxbury, we felt that we were returning the favor of being given this new home by doing all that we could to help out.

We spent one winter in West Roxbury during an unusually snowy season. We sledded down the steep streets in and around our development, skated on the frozen ponds, and had epic snowball fights. My mother would send Jeanie, Lonnie, and me to the nearest market to pick up a cherry pie and ice cream for our family to enjoy as we watched our favorite Sunday afternoon show, *Roller Derby*.

On one particularly stormy weekday, Girls' Latin dismissed the entire student body early. Kathy and I took our usual public transportation home from Dorchester and were astonished to find our father waiting in the car for us when we arrived at our Washington Street bus stop in West Roxbury. The whirling snow was getting inside our clothing and boots. By the time we clambered into the family car, we were covered with the heavy precipitation. We could not imagine how our father knew that we had been dismissed early from school, or how he knew when to be at the bus stop. He virtually never picked us up after school. Further, Kathy and I had been worried that our parents wouldn't know when to expect us or how we would make it home safely walking through the knee-deep snow. But there at the bus stop was Dad with the pre-warmed Chevy II, ready to ferry us home to Franclaire Drive.

When we got in the car with my father, we realized that he had left his job early. We had never once known that to happen with regard to my father's employment. There were no cell phones then, and not even a pay phone anywhere that we could have accessed to call my mother. She had no forewarning that we were about to embark on our snowy journey, literally all the way uphill from the bus stop to our home. Belated thanks to Dad!

An even bigger surprise awaited us when we got home. It was neither lunchtime nor suppertime, and yet my mother had a large pan of piping hot spaghetti and meat sauce ready to serve us as soon as we removed our snowy clothes and boots.

I was not (and am still not) a great fan of spaghetti and sauce, with or without meatballs. However, I must admit that on the day of that unexpected blizzard there was nothing more welcome than an early release from school, an unexpected ride from my father, and a pot of hot food prepared by my mother, who was anxiously awaiting our arrival home. It was a magical day in a magical house.

Soon, however, it became painfully apparent that something was awry on Franclaire Drive. Our house was the first in the neighborhood to be built and occupied. It was part of a much larger development that sprang up quickly across West Roxbury. Within a month of moving in, we had new neighbors next door and across the street. Shortly thereafter, more houses and families arrived. New streets were rapidly added to our development, and more new neighborhoods branched off LaGrange Street, a major road in town.

The rapidity with which the building boom struck West Roxbury was a response both to demographic changes but also to social changes in the inner city in Boston.

But a move was once again afoot. We had been in our new house for a year or so. Always sensitive to my mother's moods, I perceived increasingly that something was bothering her.

Shortly after we moved in, my parents hosted a housewarming party. We had many guests, the living room was packed with gifts for the home, and my whole family (my mother in particular) seemed ecstatic.

However, as the months went by, with all five of us kids easily settling into our new environment, I started seeing increasing frown lines on my mother's face. An extremely proud but private person, my mother would rarely reveal if something was bothering her. That is, unless it was one of us kids misbehaving. She had no hesitation then about letting her feelings be known. My mother and father were no strangers to lectures, slaps, and spankings for behavior they considered to be unacceptable.

But this was different. I began to unobtrusively watch her, trying to discern what was concerning her so much. We older kids were all so happy on Franclaire Drive. Why wasn't she?

One afternoon, my mother's favorite brother showed up at our front door. I answered it and was surprised to see him for what appeared to be a casual visit during the workweek. Instead, my mother had invited him to help her to determine why their monthly expenses, and in particular their gas bill, were so much higher than anticipated. Prior to purchasing the West Roxbury home, my parents had scrupulously examined their finances. They spoke with bankers, and they considered all anticipated monthly costs, leaving room for unexpected bills. Once in the house, they noticed with alarm that the gas bill was twice their estimated cost and continued to rise each month. They feared that they were going to be priced out of the house with little warning.

We didn't usually have much company on weekdays, so I was surprised that afternoon when I opened the door and found Uncle Joe, a career Boston Gas Company employee, waiting. He walked over to my mother and gave her a hug. She quickly sent me upstairs to check on Christine, who had awakened from her nap. I adored my little sibling, but I found it inconvenient that she was reaching out her arms to me at this time. How could I eavesdrop on my mother and Uncle Joe if I was upstairs with my little sister?

I hurriedly changed Christine's clothes and rushed back downstairs to the kitchen, hoping to catch my mother and her brother in the middle of a cup of tea and deep conversation. However, they weren't there. While I had been tending to Christine, I had heard my mother and Uncle Joe walk through the upstairs bedrooms and then down through the first floor of the house. They seemed to be looking for something. I would have been severely chastised if I asked questions that were "none of my business" (a phrase I heard often as an inquisitive kid). When I got to the kitchen with my little sister, I heard them down in the basement. Within a short while they were talking solemnly in the garage, barely audible to me since it was beneath the dining room.

I assumed that they would be back upstairs soon, so I poured fresh tea and coffee for them, and pulled out a warm coffee cake from the oven. I set the table quickly and got toys to occupy Christine. I needed to be able to surreptitiously listen to the adult conversation.

Shortly after, I got my wish. My mother and Uncle Joe emerged from the basement, but neither of them was smiling. This was particularly striking for normally jocular Uncle Joe. They sat at the table, cutting into the coffee cake and drinking their tea and coffee without question. I hovered around them, bouncing Christine on my hip to keep her quiet, and listened quietly.

Very soon, I heard the unfamiliar term "wet basement" uttered by Uncle Joe. A look at my mother's face revealed downcast eyes, a furrowed brow, and the sudden appearance of tears. My mother never cried in front of anyone! This had to be serious!

Within moments I didn't even have to try to be inconspicuous. My mother and uncle were engaged in an increasingly troubling conversation, the gist of which was that our lovely new home had serious construction problems. As my uncle described it, the house had been built so rapidly that the concrete foundation was soaking wet. It was stable enough, but the drying process was drawing off all the gas heat in the house to soak up the water. This was why the monthly expenses my parents had carefully budgeted were almost double the expected cost. My uncle estimated that the bills were going to continue to be prohibitive for at least another year before the very serious problem was remedied.

My mother gasped and said softly, "Joe, we can't afford it! How could we have anticipated this?" He assured my mother that it was not my parents' poor planning that had caused it but building contractor shortcuts.

My father came home shortly after and joined the conversation. By then I had moved on with Christine, taking her outside to play. It was no challenge for me to predict that this situation was not going to have the outcome that I dearly wanted.

By suppertime that night, my parents revealed to us kids the only option we had as a family. My parents still owned the Edwin Street house and were currently renting out the three apartments. However, one tenant and family were soon to leave. We kids were told that we would be selling the West Roxbury house as soon as possible and returning to the vacant Dorchester apartment. I had such mixed feelings: happy about returning to my Dorchester home and friends but upset about leaving Franclaire Drive.

I would still be at Girls' Latin School until the end of the current school year. Another benefit was that my commute would no longer mean a bus from West Roxbury with a transfer at Forest Hills, and then a walk up the steep hill from Ashmont Station to Girls' Latin School on Talbot Avenue.

We would all miss the single-family home and the friends we had made on Franclaire Drive and Cowing Street. We were cordial, if not quite friendly, with most of our West Roxbury neighbors. Our next-door neighbors, however, did refer to our family within our hearing as "mackerel smackers." This was a snide reference to our adhering to the Catholic decree to substitute fish for meat for Friday meals. When I had expressed anger to my mother that these neighbors were insulting us and our beliefs and practices, she quickly retorted that I had her blessing to call them "pasty Episcopalians." The shock on my face at my very proper mother's response caused her to immediately take back her words. After hearing what I had heard about the wet walls and unmanageable gas heating bills just days before, I would not have been surprised at anything that my poor mother had said in crisis mode.

Fallout from our plan to move back to Dorchester seemed to hit Kathy the hardest. Although she wouldn't admit to it, it was apparent to me that she was devastated that we were relocating. After all, as an upcoming tenth grader in an all-girls' school, Kathy had her very first boyfriend, who lived directly across the street from our house. My mother quickly perceived the developing relationship and threatened us, especially my father, not to tease my very sensitive older sister about having an intense crush on this winsome boy. It was a shock to me that my father complied. Although I was second only to my father as a teaser, even I didn't mock her sweet relationship. My mother threatened physical harm to anyone in the family who performed the singsong "Kathy and Jimmy, sitting in a tree, K-I-S-S-I-N-G!"

Jimmy and Kathy had spent many afternoons walking the neighborhood together and talking. Soon, Kathy blushed as she admitted to me that this had advanced to holding hands. They were smitten! Evenings found them sitting in his backyard exchanging words quietly in the moonlight. If my neighborhood friend Isabel came into Jimmy's yard with me and joined them (usually to mock their expressions of devotion), Kathy would chase us out, whispering that she was "going to kill us if we came back."

Since neither Kathy nor Jimmy was of age to drive, they sadly anticipated that the relationship would end when we moved back to Dorchester. As well, even if they planned on commuting to see each other, there was no way on earth that my parents would give her permission to formally "date." Reality can be unkind. The physical distance became an impenetrable barrier to the young love.

The relocation situation brought uncertainty and vulnerability to all of us, but we all began packing to go back to Edwin Street. I myself had intense ambiguity about the move. No matter what, there was loss in the situation.

As I recall this very painful event, I see how deeply it contributed to my extreme resistance to move to South Weymouth with my family after spending a year back at our Edwin Street home. This time, however, when we moved to South Weymouth, my parents sold the Edwin Street home to a trusted friend of my father's. Only then did we move. I realize now that the frequent moves in my childhood left me for a long time instinctively wanting to feel settled and secure in a home, whether it be apartment or house. It took me over 50 years to realize the deleterious effect this Fran-claire Drive debacle had on my sense of continuity and residential security! Many years have elapsed since I was a teen. I have been married for over 40 years, and we have been in our current home for over 19. I have warned my husband that I will only leave our beloved abode in a box, and it will not be a moving carton!

4

❦

A Welcome Surprise

In early September 1968, my father dropped Jeanie and me off at the front steps of South Junior High School, where we would respectively be an eighth grader and a ninth grader. He had first dropped Kathy off at Weymouth High School, where she would be a member of the junior class. As we had not yet moved into our new home on Bald Eagle Road in South Weymouth, Dad served as our chauffeur until we made our new home permanent. Once the move to Weymouth was official, we were all able to walk to our neighborhood schools, except Kathy, who took a yellow school bus for the first time in her life.

I clearly remember standing on the front steps of Weymouth South Junior High on my very first day of school. I was early, as was my habit. Fortunately, there were a few other prompt students, including one other ninth-grade girl who greeted me warmly and introduced herself. The main fact I recall about my first new classmate was that she was a petite young woman who years later became a long-distance truck driver.

The school bell announced the start of the day, and the front doors were pushed open by a throng of students. Not all rushed in. A significant number of footdraggers were apparently attempting to lengthen the summer vacation by just a few more moments.

I eagerly found my homeroom, which was directly across from the principal's office. I never needed to be sent to the principal for discipline, but it remained a good deterrent. I was assigned a seat in the first row of the classroom, allowing me to surreptitiously monitor all of the comings and goings of students and faculty in the entry hall all day long. I especially enjoyed watching the kids who had been determined to be problematic as they sat out their daytime detention on the bench reserved for this purpose in the main hall. I did a very limited amount of my own punishment time on this bench during that year, and always for talking in class.

On the very first day of school at South Junior, I was, however, called out into the hall outside my classroom. As a brand-new student, I was breathless with fear. I hadn't even had time to get into any trouble yet.

Despite my consternation, I was greeted outside my classroom door by the urbane and effusive grande dame of Weymouth public school teachers, Mrs. Alma Driscoll. Although it was not in her official capacity as an English teacher, Mrs. Driscoll had assumed the role of reading all applications for attendance at the junior high that I now attended. As we had had to write an essay describing our interests, hobbies, and personal strengths, Mrs. Driscoll knew far more about me on my first day of school than I knew about anyone in the building, except for my sister Jeanie.

Having read in my application that I played piano (although I had not indicated that I possessed any true musical ability), Mrs. Driscoll had taken it upon herself to sign me up for band and orchestra. In response to my stated history of belonging to the drama club at Girls' Latin, she informed me that I now was slated to be a member of the same club at Weymouth South Junior High. Silently, I felt that she may have oversold my so-called "talents." I had belonged to both of these organizations at Girls' Latin School, but only in bit roles. Oh well, at least she had given me opportunities for immediate participation in the student body and, thus, the chance to get to know my fellow students without much effort on my own part.

Mrs. Driscoll also assigned me to another kind and influential woman. That was Ms. Marilyn Hoffman, my new guidance counselor. When I attended my appointment with Ms. Hoffman (as hastily scheduled by Mrs. Driscoll), I was delighted to meet this lovely educator, who immediately expressed to me her "honor" of working with a former Girls' Latin School student. I didn't know at the time how this bit of knowledge obtained by my guidance counselor would affect my life in the near future.

The junior high and high school students in many Massachusetts public schools were typically assigned to either the college
preparation track, the business track, or the vocational-technical
track. For the college-track students, hundreds of brochures and
catalogs were available for perusal in the guidance office while we
waited for routine appointments, or sessions with our guidance
counselor to address an academic or social-behavioral problem.
At Girls' Latin School, because of my academic shortcomings compared to so many high-achieving students, I spent a great deal of
time in the guidance office. I continued to do so out of habit while
in the Weymouth public schools. Often, in place of a study period,
I would opt to go to the guidance office just to browse through the
college brochures. I was earning all A's in my classes and my apparent interest in college caught the attention of Ms. Hoffman. I
soon became a peer tutor, which further confirmed Ms. Hoffman's
belief that I was destined for an Ivy League acceptance when the
time came.

5

Beastly Besties

Early in my career at Weymouth's South Junior High, the best surprise of all happened in study hall, in the cafeteria.

Since the Weymouth South Junior High School building was relatively small, I had no trouble finding my homeroom. It was a pleasant surprise after all the years of Catholic school and two years of single-sex exam school with an extraordinarily challenging curriculum to suddenly be in a school where there were boys, and no one was in uniform except the lunch ladies and the janitors! I couldn't have possibly anticipated the warm feeling I had on my first day at South Junior.

The days went by pleasantly enough as I learned to negotiate the building and the schedule. I found early in the first week that I was assigned to a study hall period in the cafeteria. It was a quiet study hall, and all of my life I have had difficulty being quiet. Fortunately, I learned to write at a very young age and had mastered the art of passing notes in classes years earlier.

The students assigned to this study hall were all seated at standard cafeteria tables. I scanned my seating area for someone with whom I could chat. I quickly found an amiable female face in Barbara Donnellan.

As I didn't know her at all, I struggled to come up with a topic of conversation that might interest both of us. I quickly thought, "Music! Everyone likes music!"

I quickly penned a note about the tribute song sung by Dion

DiMucci that was a substantial American chart hit in the late 1960s. The song commemorated Abraham Lincoln, Martin Luther King, Jr., John Fitzgerald Kennedy, and Robert F. Kennedy, four American men who were assassinated in advancing the cause of freedom from slavery and discrimination in America.

I rolled the note into a ball and tossed it across the table after checking to see that no study hall monitors were nearby. The yet-to-be-met young woman caught my note, opened it, and gave me a beaming smile back.

We got brave in the cafeteria "quiet" study hall and started whispering about the song, exchanging knowledge and a definite mutual appreciation of the lyrics, and of music in general. As soon as study hall ended, we started talking endlessly to each other, both considering the possibility of being compatible enough to become friends. In truth, we were both administering each other a subtle intelligence *cum* humor assessment to decide if we might actually *want* to be friends. Apparently, we both passed, and we are still bosom buddies. She would be likely to note that we are equal in many respects, but not actual bosom-wise.

When Barbie and I walked out of the study hall together that day, we started a dialogue that has never ended. Although in the interest of accuracy, it is important to add that sometimes our discussions devolved into monologues, and at other times teasing turned into downright fighting. We got to be such close friends that we became like sisters. That is not always a good thing, given that as sister-friends we have laughed and cried together, most often with each other, but at other times because of each other.

One time, a couple of years into our friendship, we were walking together down Union Street toward her home on Constitution Avenue in South Weymouth. We had been talking and started arguing. Barbie lost her temper and hit me across the face with her new Carnaby Street-style leather cap. It felt like she had given me an open-handed slap. I reflexively, in Barbie's vernacular, "hauled off and boxed her ears." We continued on to her house where she told her mother on me. However, she neglected to tell her mother that she herself had instigated the physical part of the dispute.

I loved Barbie's mother and would never speak back to her, but I also had never been chastised by her. Barbie's mother turned to me and asked in shock, "Judy, how could you? You hurt Barbie?" I wondered at the time if Barbie's mother noticed that my face was scarlet, initially from getting slapped with the leather cap. The embarrassment of being scolded by a woman that I respected had only further reddened my cheeks. I didn't respond. Barbie, knowing that I wouldn't tell her mother what she had done to me, antagonized me further by hiding behind her mother and sticking out her tongue at me. This was becoming more of a family relationship than simply a casual friendship.

Barbie and I were competitive over so many things. One, oddly enough, was the color blue. We each felt that we "owned" the color. Our favorite song, of course, was "Love Is Blue" by Paul Mauriat.

As Barbie had taught me how to sew, we spent much time in fabric stores. One day we walked to Fitzgerald's Fabric Store on Route 53 in Weymouth to find patterns and material to make matching nightgowns. We went to the flannels section and immediately found what we wanted. Simultaneously, we reached for the blue bolt. We both had our hands on it, grabbing and tugging, trying to gain possession. The clerk came over and said, "Ladies! There is no reason to fight. This comes in pink, as well!" We both looked at her as if she had offered to solve the dispute with bloody rags. We glared at the woman and went back to struggling over the blue flannel. The clerk suggested that we toss a coin to solve the dispute. We did so. I lost. Barbie got the blue flannel. We took our packages and went our separate ways, Barbie gloating, me grumbling. At our own homes, we each cut out and sewed the nightgowns. After completing mine, I realized that the leftover fabric would be enough to make a matching accessory. I had no pattern for one, and no prior experience with my idea, but I figured out how to make a rickrack-trimmed sleeping cap to go with my (ugh!) pink nightgown.

The next night I packed the couple of items I would need for our sleepover and headed to Constitution Avenue. There would be no contest in the quality of our finished products, as Barbie had been sewing garments with her mother for years. Barbie waited to see my product so that she could duly criticize my errors. She had to admit, however, that for a beginning crafter, I had done fairly well making my nightgown. Since we had used identical patterns, any errors on mine would appear egregious compared to Barbie's fine work. However, she graded mine B work, explaining that the letter stood for "beginner." I pulled out my matching sleeping cap, and she got flustered. Barbie demanded to know when I had gotten the pattern for it. I told her that I had simply improvised with the fabric and trim that I had left over from the nightgown. Instead of concluding that in our own ways we had each "won" the unspoken competition, we both sulked. Barbie's mother came into the bedroom and admired our work profusely, thus calming the storm. Fortunately, as the days and years passed in our lives, we lost our competitiveness and instead shared in each other's happiness and sadness, thus laying the foundation for a 50-plus-year friendship.

There was one more instance where Barbie's mother stepped in and resolved a dispute that had arisen between us.

Barbie and I were both born in September of 1954, me on the twelfth and she on the nineteenth. I am exactly a week older than she is, and she has reminded me of that every September for the past half-century-plus. We always gave each other birthday presents until our later years—when the gift was staying in each other's lives.

When we were still scrappy teens, however, we had gone to a new gift shop in Columbian Square. We both immediately fell in love with the same pair of earrings. They were sterling silver dangling earrings with a blue bead with green accents, encircled by a silver hoop. Once again, we got into a bitter argument in the small store, both of us refusing to choose a different pair. Barbie won again. She happily paid for the earrings, and I stormed out. However, in our haste, we had both overlooked a second pair of nearly identical earrings. The second pair had red accents on the blue bead. My birthday was coming up and, not surprisingly, I was at Barbie's house on the morning of September 12. Barbie's mother came into the room with a small, wrapped box in her hand, and handed it to me saying, "Happy birthday, Jude!" I was stunned to receive a gift but thrilled when I opened it. Inside the box was the second pair of earrings that Barbie and I had not noticed. The sterling silver earrings with the blue bead with red accents was nestled in cotton in the little box. Barbie had apparently related our latest argument to her mother, who took the time, without telling Barbie, to go back to the same gift store and find the second pair. I was walking on air with delight.

Mrs. Donnellan—you were a formative presence in both of our lives. Thank you! You may well have saved two competitive teenage girls from juvenile hall on multiple occasions.

As time progressed, Barb and I became what might be appropriately termed "Beastly Besties"! We loved each other most of the time, but we acted like prizefighters at other times. The stakes might be low or high, but when our Irish temperaments led to one-upmanship, we were ultimately both going down.

I was still new to Weymouth and had a number of friendly acquaintances, but my prior lifelong friends had been left behind in Dorchester. Shortly after meeting Barb, she introduced me to Michael, a boy from her neighborhood with whom she had grown up. To Barb, Michael was a good friend. Michael, however, was hopelessly devoted to Barb. I quickly became the newest member of the threesome, but there was built-in favoritism in our relationships. As long as Barb and Michael had known each other, he thought she could do no wrong. Thus, as we all spent more and more time together, the inevitable disputes developed. None of us were strangers to a good argument, but I always lost whatever struggle was at hand.

Michael tipped the scales in Barb's favor constantly. He couldn't help it. He had been enamored of her since long before I knew either of them. When I became friends with Barb at the beginning of the ninth grade, he became my bonus friend, but his loyalties were always with Barb.

Barb and I often acted like spatting siblings, and the dynamic was influenced by Michael's deep loyalty to his childhood friend and neighbor. We could have the best time together, or else we could be nearly at each other's throats.

Most people have physical characteristics they would prefer be different. For Barb, it was her hair. She had light brown hair that was always perfectly coiffed. It was apparent that she spent time each night taking measures to ensure that her hair did not, in her perspective, look "frizzy." I never saw frizz, and she promised me that on a weekend she would let her hair stay in its natural state so that I could see for myself why it was so unattractive in her own estimation.

Barb also had a stunning figure, often telling her hippy best friend (me) that *she* occasionally was asked to model. My own disproportionate physical attributes negated that possibility for me. However, there is often balance in nature. Barb did, at times, allow her light brown hair to remain in its natural state on weekends, and I reluctantly admitted that, yes, her hair was actually frizzy.

As the societal ideal in the late 1960s and into the 1970s was straight, long, blond hair, I won on that count. I didn't make much of my attribute because we were always taught in my family that bragging was a sin, and if we had a God-given gift, we should accept it humbly. But my hair apparently bothered Barb more than I could possibly have known, and she engaged Michael in what she laughingly later called "just a joke."

One afternoon, the three of us were sitting on the front steps. I was on the bottom step, closest to the front walk, and Barb and Michael were sitting two steps above and behind me.

Barb made an excuse to go into her house, and Michael and I continued to chat. She returned and took her place again beside Michael. As it was a warm summer day, I was wearing sandals. Barb suddenly said, "Judy, you have weird-shaped toes." I snapped back, "I do *not*!" She laughed and said, "Wow, I never noticed how weird they are."

Michael instantly corroborated Barb's accusations, and added, "Judy, look closely at your crooked toes!" Innocently, I bent my head forward and over my feet to disprove their accusation. I suddenly felt a tugging at my hair, and Michael laughed uproariously as Barb reached in front of me to show me the eight-inch lock of hair and the scissors with which she had snipped it as I had leaned forward over my own (straight) toes!

I screamed and yelled at both of them. The more I objected to their assault on me, the more they laughed. I jumped on my bike and rode home in an absolute fury. I was determined never to speak to either of them again.

I got home and showed my mother. I was too angry to explain calmly what had happened to me. I also didn't expect any sympathy because both Barb's mother and my own were getting rather used to our love/hate relationship.

However, my mother just said, "Long hair needs periodic trims to keep it healthy. Let me just even this out and your hair will look even healthier and thicker." I couldn't have asked for kinder, more reassuring words.

Although I had sworn that I would never associate with Barb and Michael after what I considered to be their atrocious assault on me, I got back on my bike and returned to Constitution Avenue. Both looked stunned as they watched me return, tossing my blonde hair. They were stymied. I gloated to them, "It is so cute. My little sister Christine told me that now I look even more like Lady Godiva!"

With that I gave a toss of my crowning glory and smiled smugly at them both.

This kind of behavior among the three of us went on for years. We were the best of friends, and the worst of friends, depending on the moment. One factor never changed, however, and that was that Michael would defend Barb to the death if there was any ill will between us. I didn't realize how much it bothered me that I was always "third friend out," but it apparently built up over the years.

It finally all came down to an event that shocked not only the three of us, but our entire tenth grade class as well.

Michael and I both participated in drama throughout our school years in Weymouth. When we were in the tenth grade, there were try-outs for short individual scenes from Shakespearean plays. Michael and I both tried out for one of many of the scenes. Strangely enough, Michael and I were cast together in *The Taming of the Shrew.*

Our scene had Katherine retaliating for cruel treatment following her willful fighting with her brutal husband Petruchio. My role, as Kate, in the one short scene, was to rebuke Petruchio, objecting to his cruel attempts to "tame" me as his outspoken wife. The role called for me to excoriate Petruchio and then to slap him. Unfortunately, the character playing Petruchio was Michael. This was not a good time for us to act out this scene in front of the entire tenth-grade audience. I still hadn't forgotten the hair-cutting incident and was harboring resentment of which I was unaware.

Michael and I practiced our roles diligently and finally took the stage on the designated day to act out this scene in front of the entire tenth grade. Teachers and administrators were in the crowd as well, since no classes were scheduled during the performances.

I didn't realize how much I was still holding onto my vexation at Michael. When Michael spoke Petruchio's words to me, and the scene called for me to slap Petruchio's face, I hauled off and belted Michael so hard that the entire audience gasped!

There was a discernible pause while the horrified student body and the faculty collected themselves. Even I recognized that my enraged slapping of Michael might be termed an "assault on school property." The principal and others ultimately decided that it was merely a case of "overacting" and counseled me appropriately. I was never invited to act in any stage performances again while at school in Weymouth.

After school, I apologized profusely to Michael and was relieved that he accepted. Barb was still mad at me, but Michael intervened and calmly reminded us that we had all done some pretty regretful things to each other in the course of our friendship. It was enough for Barb that Michael was graceful to me, for the moment at least. We continued to be friends for life, and one of the three of us was often on the outs with the other two. Fortunately, all in all we were united in our true friendship and had many years of joy, happiness, and turbulence during our adolescent years. I can't say that all the rest has been smooth sailing, but for the vast majority of our time together, our lives have been enriched by the camaraderie.

6

With a License to Drive

At Weymouth South High School, I was a particular favorite of the math teacher Mr. Miller because of my facility with algebra. As well, as an eleventh grader, I relieved him of his own extra school duties by staying after school voluntarily to tutor classmates in the tricky subject.

Driver's education classes were available for students at no cost at South High School, and it just so happened that Mr. Miller was also the driver's education instructor. Since there were a limited number of openings for the high-demand course, opportunities for "driver's ed" were essentially limited to twelfth graders. But Mr. Miller remembered that he got to leave school early each day that he wasn't teaching driver's education, since I was doing his after-school duties with my algebra tutoring.

One day he came to me and said, "Judith. I want to talk to you about something." I knew that I hadn't done anything wrong (in this particular instance), so I just looked at him blankly. He paused for a moment and then said, "How would you like to take driver's education now?" I almost screamed with excitement but kept my calm. He said, "I have two available slots." As if this wasn't enough of a privilege, I was my usual bold self and answered, "I will take driver's education if you let my friend Barbie into the course too." Either flummoxed by my nerviness or else thinking Barbie would be a pleasant and cooperative student, he readily acquiesced.

Thus, lessons commenced. We both had already obtained our learner's permits, so we were prepared for formal driving lessons.

Our parents were delighted with the opportunity we had been given, as Barbie and I both had part-time jobs after school and usually needed rides to and from our jobs.

In the course of our taking driver's education, my parents decided that they needed a new and larger car. They bought a red Ford Pinto wagon for my mother and sold the 1967 Marina Blue Chevy II sedan to me. I couldn't have been happier. Now I could drive myself and my friends anywhere I wanted. I mean, I could "work more hours per week!" Actually, I did both.

When Mr. Miller deemed that Barbie and I had successfully completed our driver's education course, he took the two of us out together and directed me into the driver's seat. He told me to go south on Route 3 toward Cape Cod. We were curious as to why he would take us on this route that was not a scheduled part of our training. Once I was driving at the posted speed on the highway, Mr. Miller told me to merge into the high-speed lane. Once I was there, he put his left foot on my right foot and pressed down hard on the pedal, causing me to be speeding. Scared, I asked him what he was doing. He answered, "You kids are going to be all over the roads once you get your license. None of my driving students are going to start speeding without learning *how* to!" I was shocked but maintained control of the car. He had me drive at this rate for about 15 miles and then had me pull off the ramp and get out of the car. He then demanded that Barbie replace me in the driver's seat. Knowing what was coming, she jumped out and attempted to walk home, but it was just too far! She got back into the driver's education car.

Barbie took the wheel and was directed to reverse course, going back to Weymouth via Route 3 North. He did the same to her as he had done to me: he placed his left foot atop her right foot and then put the pedal to the metal. We were both terrified, but we made it back to the school, and he signed and gave us both a certificate of successful completion of our driving training education.

Our road tests were next. I passed, and then it was Barbie's turn. She did an 11-point turn in place of the three-point turn that she was directed to do, but the registry officer who tested us was kind and passed the two of us. We both got our driver's licenses on the first try!

We hurried all the way home from school to Bald Eagle Road,

where my own personal car was waiting for me in the driveway. My mother was standing at the front door with baby Scott in her arms when we ran screaming onto our property. I threw my books in the house and said to my mother, "We passed our driving tests! We'll be back!"

I should be embarrassed to say that the very first place that we went with our hot-off-the-press temporary licenses was to Burger King, on Washington Street in Weymouth. In celebration, we each got a Whopper with cheese, a large serving of french fries, onion rings, and a Diet Coke—as if the lower amount of sugar in the drink made any difference in our total caloric consumption!

Satisfied by our meals as well as our success in getting our licenses, we drove back to my house. My poor mother was still standing in the doorway, holding Scott. She had been too paralyzed with fear to leave the spot until the two of us got home, sated *and* safe!

I was limited by my parents to driving only in Weymouth, and most of the time I just didn't really have the desire to challenge them. All my friends, my school, and my job were in Weymouth. Not long after, Barbie and I and our other friends who had their driver's licenses began to wander farther afield.

Just months after we both began to drive independently, the thoughtful Donnellan parents took Barbie, her younger sister, Cathy, and me to the Lord Fox restaurant in Foxborough, Massachusetts, a site known for its sumptuous Sunday buffets and upscale wedding receptions. Because Barbie and I celebrate our birthdays exactly one week apart in September, and I was at Barbie's house as much as my family home, Barbie's kind mother got into the habit of always celebrating my birthday when they celebrated Barbie's. Thus, I was graciously invited to join the family for brunch that Sunday morning.

On arrival, I was in absolute awe. Coming from a family with seven kids and parents with strict food portions and rules, I had never been in a situation where not only was I allowed to choose anything that I wanted, but I could keep going back for more.

Barbie's parents were very liberal with their time, as well, for the two greedy teens who felt that one would only get their money's worth if one went up to the buffet repeatedly for the unlimited offerings. Barbie and I, likely embarrassing her parents and younger sister, were not shy about filling our plates with seconds, then thirds

of bacon, waffles, omelets, hash brown potatoes, cranberry muf-
fins, and chocolate croissants. We washed it all down with cup after
cup of coffee. It was amazing! No one, absolutely *no one*, told us
that we had had enough! Finally, we were both almost too stuffed to
move. We waddled out to the car, spread across the wide back seat,
and, to younger sister Cathy's consternation, snoozed as her father
drove home.

I was chattering to my parents as I bounced in through the
front door, breathlessly describing our delightful experience. It is
safe to say that my parents were less than pleased with the amount
that I bragged that I had consumed at that one meal.

Months later, Barb and I both got our permanent driver's
licenses and together headed out of town one Sunday morning after
early Mass. The destination was determined, but the directions
were unknown to either of us. All we were sure of was that we were
headed to Foxborough. As one might anticipate, after a few false
starts, we found our way to the glitzy facility.

Since our previous trip to the restaurant, we had spent many
hours fondly reminiscing about the Miracle of the Endless Meal at
the Lord Fox.

We arrived and parked right by the front door, nearly beating the server getting to a table close to the food array, and lustily
waited to hear the words, "You may now serve yourselves at the
buffet." The waitress all but whirled in place as we scooted rapidly
around her to get to the food. We were there for hours. We'd eat,
have some coffee, get more food, take a trip to the ladies' restroom,
and start over again.

When we finally arrived back at my house, my parents demanded to know where we had been for so long. Matter of factly, I
answered that we had gone to the Lord Fox for brunch. My parents,
perplexed as to how we had negotiated our way there—as fairly new
drivers—shook their heads in consternation. My father looked at
the two of us, knowing he had solved the mystery of our traversing
the unfamiliar route. He said, "So the two of you just followed your
noses." He then added that it was likely that Barbie and I would be
unwelcome guests at the facility in the future, as we had most likely
"eaten up all their profits for the week."

Having our driver's licenses brought us places independently. We didn't get into trouble with our parents necessarily for

venturing out for innocent fun and games, but instead for consistently forgetting to tell them where we were going and how long we would be gone.

Prior to obtaining our driver's licenses, we enjoyed our summer forays to the Weymouth Fairgrounds. For over 100 years, the Weymouth Fair was conveniently located in South Weymouth, and thus a short walk from our homes. The fair had long featured horse racing, athletic contests, midway rides, livestock shows, and 4-H contests. Over the fair's eight-day run in 1970 alone, more than 100,000 people attended the event.

Barb, Michael, and I were there among the many patrons. It was highly likely that we could be found at least once each day of the fair on a wooden bench, slobbering down our sizzling hot-fried dough. Most people preferred the fried dough sprinkled with powdered sugar, but the melted drops of butter staining our clothing clearly indicated our preference.

Unfortunately, the Weymouth Fair disappeared from its longtime home on Park Avenue in South Weymouth. The last fair was held in 1972. It closed for good shortly after, giving way to a housing development of primarily single-family homes. Those of us living in South Weymouth during the era of the Weymouth Fair still slip and call those now long-established neighborhoods "the Fairgrounds houses."

While we missed the Weymouth Fairgrounds, since we were all legally licensed to drive, we would go to Hull's Nantasket Beach and Paragon Park for swimming among rollicking waves and having our share of carnival fun at the amusement site. At Paragon, Michael and I challenged each other to contests involving who could ride the Giant Roller Coaster more times in a row. Whoever vomited first lost! We felt a little old riding the Philadelphia Toboggan Company Carousel with the hand-crafted horses, but it was a good way of settling down after what was often misnamed "the biggest roller coaster in the world." We occasionally rode the bumper cars, often violating the rule of avoiding head-on collisions. Among the many rides at Paragon Park, the three of us agreed that the best of all was the Matterhorn, a wild ride that went rapidly and roughly up and down, backward and forward, and side to side on an oscillating track. We *loved* it. I will never forget the accompanying soundtrack that played "Mony Mony" as we spun and dipped.

In between the rides, we strolled the boardwalk, scarfing down fried clams and saltwater taffy. And finally, trying to settle our still-shaking bodies and full stomachs, we strolled through the penny arcade before making our way back to the parking lot for the relatively brief drive back to Weymouth.

In retrospect, had I known about all that *was* available to us in Weymouth and beyond, I might not have fought my parents so hard about moving out of Dorchester. Scratch that. I most definitely would still have objected—knowing me—despite the fact that we had a good life in Weymouth and beyond.

7

ℒ

Finger Lakes, New York

One summer I was invited by Barbie's mother to go with the family on vacation to the Finger Lakes region in New York. I was stunned to be asked. I wondered if Barbie's parents thought that I was actually one of their kids, since I was at their house so often. But I caught on that it was a legitimate invitation to join them and Michael's family on this trip, as both families had gone together for years. I was stunned that my parents gave me permission, as long as I had my work shifts at Bea's Bakery covered. I did.

While we were in the Finger Lakes, Barbie, Michael, and I learned how to water-ski on a lake. I am not, and have never been, physically adept, except for riding my bike all over Dorchester, and later all over the South Shore.

But at the lake there was a red-headed young man about our age. Barbie and I, and even Michael, mocked a fair number of people behind their backs. We never ever did so in a way that anyone knew that we were quietly (but rudely) ridiculing them. However, we were being unpleasant teens merely for each other's entertainment. This young guy not only had red hair, but it was very curly, as was his facial hair. I don't know which one of us christened him "Freddy Frizz-top." But we laughed ourselves silly when we saw him for the first few times. We became a little less amused when we were able to observe his proficiency with waterskiing.

Before long, Barbie was sitting beside him on the dock flirting

with him. I was annoyed because we had been scorning him together and now she was friends with Freddy. Michael disliked
Freddy because Barb had always been the object of Michael's desire. Soon after, the three of us were hanging around with Freddy
on a daily basis.

Freddy had little choice among the friends he made at the lake.
As an only child, he had no siblings to keep him company, and others who vacationed on the Finger Lakes were generally there for
short periods of time.

When his father was available, he would operate the controls of
their motorboat until Freddy graciously rose from the water on his
skis and athletically conquered the entire lake. We started joining
Freddy on the dock daily, and soon after he offered to teach us all
to water-ski. We didn't call him names behind his back anymore.

As clumsy as I have always been, I did actually water-ski during that week. Barbie and Michael took to the sport immediately; I
was still nervous, but I did it.

By the end of the two weeks, Barbie had changed her opinion
of Freddy radically, and she thinks that I don't know, but she com-
municated with him by phone and letters for a number of years
after. Poor Michael. Another competitor for Barbie's affections.
However, no one could really ever take Michael's place as her first
and lifetime best male friend.

Aside from the water skiing, two more noteworthy events took
place during our two weeks in the Finger Lakes. Both were poten-
tially life-threatening but turned out well.

Very early one morning, Michael's dad, Mr. Thornton, was
dozing lightly but came to immediately when he smelled gas.
Everyone else was sleeping deeply, with snores emanating from
most of the bedrooms in the spacious cabin. Mr. Thornton jumped
up quietly, and rapidly assessed a carbon monoxide leak. Without
causing a panic, he went from room to room, stating firmly but
gently, "Get out of the cabin now!" No one questioned him. His
voice indicated that this was *not* the time for any pause in our
evacuation. We all walked outside and away from the cabin, and it
was then he told us that there was a carbon monoxide leak.

Red blood cells pick up carbon monoxide (CO) more quickly
than they pick up oxygen. When one inhales CO, the body replaces
the oxygen in blood with CO. Every year, at least 430 people die in

the United States from accidental CO poisoning, and about 50,000 people in the US visit the emergency department due to accidental CO poisoning.

By waking us and sending us outside and into the fresh air immediately, Mr. Thornton's actions enabled us to take in more oxygen and reduce the risk of suffering further effects, including death. Our quiet hero called the fire department immediately after ensuring that we were all outside. Only then did he and Mr. Donnellan go back into the cabin to open all the windows and doors and allow atmospheric oxygen to replace the carbon monoxide. I have been grateful since that day for both men's rapid and life-saving actions.

The final significant event was the appearance of a bear cub in the tree just outside our cabin on our very last day. Barbie and I had very mixed feelings about leaving the Finger Lakes district. We got up early, packed, and went to spend the last two hours or so outside in the woods. Barbie noticed movement in a tree we were under. She looked up and cried, "There's a bear cub right there!"

We were constantly pranking each other, so I didn't believe her at first. She ran in and got Michael, and he grabbed our cameras and came out. We started snapping pictures as the cub climbed around in the tree. The adorable animal went from one branch to another, allowing us (unintentionally) a number of different camera views of the baby bear. We were very excited! Suddenly, Barbie's mother came out and called to us, "Get away from the cub! Bear cubs are never alone! The mother has to be nearby, and she will *not* appreciate you threatening her baby!" Hmmm . . . we hadn't thought of that! Neighbors in close-by cabins heard us excitedly exclaiming about the cub in the tree just feet away. They joined in calling out their warnings to us to stay as far away from the cub as we could. Another long-term vacationer in the Finger Lakes recreation area said that it had been over 20 years since a cub had made its way so close to the cabins.

Barbie, Michael, and I continued to look back fondly on the cuteness of our Finger Lake friends. I meant the bear cub. Barbie meant Freddy. Michael still meant Barbie.

8

⤸

Dancing with the Protestants

When we first moved to South Weymouth, I discovered that many of my new classmates and friends were Protestant. This was quite a difference after having been raised in predominantly Irish Catholic Dorchester.

Having come from this environment, we generally did not have a lot of interaction with people of other faiths or ethnic identities. Unfortunately, the nuns forbade us from associating with Protestants, or any other non-Catholics for that matter.

In the two academic years (1966–1967 and 1967–1968) that I attended Girls' Latin School in Dorchester, I intermingled with students of all races, religions, and ethnic practices and beliefs. When we moved in 1968 to South Weymouth, Irish Catholics still made up a significant percentage of the town residents. Yet a notable number of Protestant families lived in our part of the town as well. Many of those attended Church of the Holy Nativity, a short distance from Columbian Square.

Saint Francis Xavier Catholic Church on Pleasant Street served the spiritual needs of the South Weymouth Catholic community. Saint Francis Xavier School was attended by a small proportion of Catholic students in South Weymouth, but the vast majority of students in the town attended the highly rated public schools.

Many Catholic students in South Weymouth attended both Confraternity of Christian Doctrine (for religious education) and Catholic Youth Organization (CYO) within the Saint Francis Xavier parish.

Especially relevant for me was that many of my non-Catholic Weymouth friends were members of the Masonic organizations DeMolay (for boys) and Rainbow (for girls).

For my friends and for me, Holy Nativity had far more interesting and exciting social events, especially dances, for its members than our church did. Guests not belonging to the Holy Nativity Church or its youth organizations were welcome.

Especially popular were the Holy Nativity Church dances. They had live bands made up of DeMolay members, most of whom attended the Weymouth schools. As soon as I moved to Weymouth and began establishing friendships in the schools, I began to be invited to DeMolay dances. That was impetus for conflict at home.

I was allowed to go to CYO dances held at the Saint Francis Xavier parish hall but was forbidden to go to Holy Nativity dances simply because they were not Catholic. I argued loudly and persistently with my parents about their refusal to let me go to Holy Nativity. I pointed out to them that the CYO dances were not necessarily religiously segregated, and, also, they weren't much fun. So, I stopped telling them which dances I was attending on a given night out.

If my parents determined through devious means (such as telephone calls to both Saint Francis Rectory and to Holy Nativity Church) which church was sponsoring a dance on a given night, I was only allowed to go to the Saint Francis events. Additionally, I was able to attend dances held at the Weymouth public schools. However, I finally found the golden ticket that allowed me to go to any church or school-sponsored dance.

In an era in which equal rights by race, age, gender, sex, religion, nationality, disability status, and numerous other characteristics of individuals and groups within society were being fought for in the United States and elsewhere, I found my parents' vulnerable spot.

As highly intelligent individuals who demanded that their children be informed, knowledgeable, spiritual, *and* dedicated to human rights issues, I called them on their failure. When the next argument arose regarding my invitation to a Holy Nativity dance, they immediately said **"No!"**. I retorted, "So you are saying that you are in favor of discrimination?!"

I had to watch my step as my parents were definitely in favor of slapping fresh kids. But my accusation gave them pause. They capitulated. "Fine," they said. "But be home by nine o'clock." That wasn't going to happen. I pleasantly reminded them that they had given me permission to spend the night at Barbie's house. They were stuck. They couldn't rescind my privilege of staying overnight after a dance at Holy Nativity Church, as permission would not have been taken back without cause if the dance was at Saint Francis.

My parents had come to know Barbie through her frequent presence at my house. If Barbie was not at my house, I was at hers. My parents never knew for sure whether they had six kids at home at any given time, or eight. The seventh child, Nancy, would be born in February of 1970. So, there was in more ways than one an ever-changing number of kids in our house, both because of my parents' own baby boom, which spanned 17 years, and the constant sleepovers by us, our friends, and our many cousins at each other's houses.

My parents had significant apprehension about Kathy and I having driver's licenses. At the same time, my mother and father realized how much more we could do for the household as drivers. My mother would be able to pass off the onerous task of grocery shopping, for example. I insisted that that job go to Kathy, once she was working in a supermarket. I was left a plethora of other errands to do once I got my own license, and stiff curfews for evenings out of the house, but we were teens now and fully enjoying the increasing tastes of freedom from parental supervision!

9

Introduction to the World of Work: Bea's Bakery and W. T. Grants

My parents were firm believers in the adage that "idle hands are the devil's workshop." In other words, one must always be constructively busy to keep one from getting into trouble. As the second-oldest in a family of seven children, I don't recall ever just relaxing when I lived at home. The three oldest girls, in particular, were never allowed to be inactive. There were always babies to take care of, neighbors' children to take care of, food preparation and cleaning up, household tasks, and errands to be done. For many years, I used to have to hide from my mother in order to read. While my parents did encourage reading, the time allowed for that was between climbing into bed at night and falling asleep. However, I found ways between chores to get my reading in. It was uncomfortable hiding under my father's car, but it worked.

Not long after moving to South Weymouth, Kathy got a job at Bea's Bakery in Columbian Square. She never really said much about the job other than that the pay was terrible. The primary work, serving the customers, was relatively easy, except for having to empty and scrub the display cases every night. But the back-room work was odious—it meant hand-scrubbing all of the baking pans every night. Kathy kept a lookout for other jobs and soon scored a much desired but hard to acquire job at Purity Supreme Supermarket.

To my surprise, although I shouldn't have been, my parents quickly realized that Kathy's moving on meant that there was an opening at Bea's Bakery. Within hours of Kathy giving her notice, my parents had called Gianni, the owner, and volunteered me for the job. He hired me without even interviewing me. It was well worth it to him to hire *anybody* willing to work for $1.30 per hour. I had mixed feelings when I heard that I was to be gainfully employed: I would be earning money, but I would have less time to hang around with Barb, Michael, and others. I had a problem that needed solving, so as soon as I started work at Bea's, I volunteered Barbie for the next part-time opening at the bakery with me.

Gianni thought it was an easy solution; after all, he didn't have to look for a new part-timer, and this person was already familiar with the requirements of the job, having visited me at work numerous times.

For the most part, Barb and I had a great deal of fun on the job. The biggest disadvantage at Bea's Bakery was that we ate as much of the delicious Italian pastry as we sold. Another aspect that was both good and bad was that if the schedule called for only one evening worker, we were alone in the bakery and unsupervised for three hours. Part of the evening job was to put all the cash from the register into a banker's cloth bag and hide it in the freezer, lock up the bakery, take the key home, and return it to Bea's before eight the following morning.

There were a number of times that I felt uncomfortable working alone at night, especially as very close to the bakery was a park that served as a neighborhood hangout. Not all of those who used the park were there for the swing sets and tennis courts. The drug scene was a big part of life for many. We had stragglers in the bakery from the park often enough to be scary. They came into the bakery at night looking for free food, to use the employee bathroom, or to beg for money. Most often the only thing that stood between the full cash register and the would-be-thief was an adolescent female clerk working alone. Fortunately, we had a neighborhood police officer whose beat was Columbian Square. He assigned himself as Barbie's and my protector when we were working evenings. He dropped into the bakery frequently during our shifts, and just his presence alone was enough of a deterrence to anyone with bad intentions toward us or the bakery itself. But not all threats came from strangers.

Of the other young women who worked at Bea's, some worked with Barbie, or with me, or they worked alone when neither of us were scheduled. Tiffany was another part-timer. She was a very attractive 17-year-old who was worrisome to me as much because of her naivete as my own caution about potential predators.

Bea's Bakery had a gumball machine right inside the front door, as did many stores at the time. Gumball machines attracted little kids walking by, and when they ran from their mothers right into the bakery, their mothers quickly followed to retrieve their children. Once in the store to appease the offspring begging for gumballs and prizes in the machine, the mothers couldn't help but be enticed by the smell of the baking goods. This worked out for the kids and for Bea's. While there was virtually no profit in the gumballs, the mothers often left with boxes of pastries and freshly baked and sliced bread as well.

The gumball machine was routinely serviced by an outside vendor. This man was a reprehensible jerk I could not tolerate. Gus, the gumball man, came in once a week to empty the machine of all the pennies and refill the gum and little prizes. He would routinely take the cash into the back room of the bakery to weigh, rather than to count, the pennies, and then to roll them for deposit to the bank. Each time he came in, I avoided him. To me, he was a slimy guy, always making suggestive comments and looking the young female employees up and down. I was outright rude to him to prevent him from even trying to interact with me.

Tiffany, however, was tall and slender with a noticeably large bust. She wore a short, tight uniform, and acted flirtatiously with Gus. She seemed to thrive on attention from him, even when I suggested to Tiffany that his attention to her body was inappropriate, and his language offensive.

When we female clerks were working in the front of the store, we had to go out back frequently for supplies. We only spent any significant time in the back room when it was time to scrub the baking pans prior to closing. Otherwise, the vast majority of our time was out front. However, when the gumball man came, he spent a brief amount of time in the front, flirting with whomever was working.

He got icy responses from me, so he stopped bothering and focused on others who were receptive to his inappropriate attention.

However, each time he walked behind the side counters on his way to the back room, he'd gratuitously rub his body against any clerks at the display cases. I began to notice that on days he came in when I was working with Tiffany, she would place herself by the side case so that he would have to pass her closely. She seemed to not realize that she was playing right into his hands. I took her aside one day and said, "Tiffany, he's a disgusting creep. Please don't flirt with him. He'll take advantage of you." She laughed and dismissed my concern. After I witnessed him rubbing his body against her as he made his way to the back room, I warned her again about his inappropriate behavior, and she retorted that he "meant nothing by it."

One day, a number of customers came in at once. Tiffany and I were working, and I began to wait on the throng. Within minutes, I noticed that Tiffany was not in the front room. I thought that maybe she had gone out back to wash pans early, but I needed her help out front. I called her and got no response. I waited on customers until the store was empty.

Finally, all the customers were gone, and I stopped to take a quick break. I heard rapid shuffling as the gumball man hurried out of the store, glancing guiltily in my direction. Minutes after the door slammed behind him, Tiffany came barreling out of the back room, ran out the front door, and threw something out into the street. I chased after her to find out what had upset her. She screamed, "*Filthy bastard!* He touched me! He thrust his tongue down my throat as he groped me! *Bastard!!* And then the son-of-a bitch shoved a bunch of coins into my uniform pocket and said, 'Thank you! It was worth the money!'"

That was when she threw the change as hard as she could into Columbian Street just to rid it from her possession. I wanted to comfort her because she had been victimized. But she was too humiliated and simply left. She never came back to work at the bakery again.

The penny man stopped servicing the gumball machine after the assault on Tiffany. It is unlikely that it was guilt that propelled him to quit, as this sexually predatory activity was a common phenomenon, even in our relatively sheltered lives. And such egregious behavior would have been blamed on Tiffany by many. It was *not* her fault, and yet she suffered dire emotional consequences. Looking back, we were both complicit in staying silent about the gumball man despite the negative emotional effects suffered by Tiffany. Unfortunately, in such cases, victims are nearly always blamed for "looking too sexy," "behaving too provocatively," and even "asking for it."

Soon after, I decided that I did not want to be alone in the bakery alone at night anymore, even with the supervision of our own "Officer Friendly" in Columbian Square. Upon the urging of friends from my neighborhood and school, I applied for a job at W. T. Grants department store in Weymouth.

The hourly rate of pay was higher, and there was far more variety in working in different departments of the store compared to a two-room bakery. Most of all, I liked the safety of having a store full of shoppers and employees surrounding me whenever I worked. There was also more of an opportunity to meet people of differing ages and life circumstances, as well as the opportunity to learn different skills, depending on which department I was assigned to over the two years that I worked at Grants.

Another aspect of working with such a variety of people turned out to be a double-edged sword. Before I worked at Grants, I had occasional boyfriends. These were limited to people I met either in my neighborhood or at school. They tended to be close in age to me, at similar life stages. At Grants, three female co-workers became close friends. Deirdre, Colleen, and Maura were a year ahead of me in school and had substantially more flirting and dating experience than I did.

Not really understanding the culture of work in the late 1960s and into the 1970s and beyond, I had no prior knowledge that the workplace was also typically a place where people formed relationships—both friendship bonds and different levels of intimate attachments. The predatory aspect of the older, more opportunistic would-be-partners was one type of behavior that I saw taking place over and over. Grants, as a formal organization, had a "no fraternization policy," meaning that intimate relationships between lower-status workers and supervisors of any sort were strictly prohibited. However, that did not mean that this situation did not occur all of the time, at work and outside of work.

One factor that made "fraternization" an even more likely scenario was that Grants yearly brought in about a dozen young college graduates who had completed the company's management training program. They tended to be in their early twenties and were almost exclusively single men. Each summer, the new "crop" of trainees arrived, ready to work, to learn to become a Grants store manager—and to party.

What made this situation even more fraught was that for its nonprofessional labor force, Grants had no shortage of primarily female employees. They spanned high-school-aged students, young mothers working part-time to support their children, and the corps of loyal older women workers who had dedicated their lives to W. T. Grants. Finally, the last category of workers at Grants were males of all ages lacking college educations. They were employed both full- and part-time and made low- to mid-level salaries. Few of them advanced beyond department management level, as the company maintained the ongoing management training program until W. T. Grants went out of business in 1976 after 70 years of operation throughout the United States.

Humans tend to be social animals, and the way of socializing most common at the Weymouth Grants was through surreptitious fraternization. This, in my experience, for example, included a store manager who was not far short of retirement age when he began dating a woman in her forties who was employed as a credit department clerk. The relationship, according to store gossip, was particularly noticeable because they became careless about being seen in each other's company in front of the store's employees. She was also observed to spend a very significant amount of time during her workday either accompanying him on his rounds through the store or joining him in his office for excessive amounts of time relative to what was allowed for employee breaks.

The factor that was most commented on as being unfair was that this store manager was breaking a primary rule of W. T. Grants in his very visible relationship with an employee of a significantly lower status than his in the company. If anyone were to be fired as a result of the illicit relationship, we all speculated that it would be the woman.

And finally, most startling to those who observed the close public interaction between the two, was that the female employee was almost an exact physical replica of his wife, who was in her sixties (as he was). The couple became so lax about their constant togetherness that there was an all-employee meeting after work one night, and his wife came in to meet him, expecting to go out socializing with her husband after work.

Not unexpectedly, virtually no employees were focused on what was to be a workplace presentation of Grants quarterly productivity. Instead, most of us stared open-mouthed, watching the manager while he talked, bracketed by the two tall, slender women with short blond hair and angry looks on their faces. The wife "won," according to the gamblers in the group who had taken bets on the eventual outcome. As expected, the much younger credit clerk and former companion of the manager did not work at Grants after that night.

The bigger problem was that this tolerance for flouting the rules of non-fraternization with employees of inferior job status ran throughout the chain of command, and it was not necessarily initiated by just the male employees.

When each new cohort of management trainees arrived on scene in July of each year, women of all ages who also worked in the store eyed the new hires for dating potential. At first, the group of mostly young male college graduates followed the strict protocol about which they had been instructed. The management trainees resisted dating current store employees during their probationary period, but when those three months elapsed, there was a great deal of pairing off. This was further enhanced by the encouragement of groups of employees who found themselves on the evening shift. It was common practice for many of the employees, regardless of age, gender, role, or marital status, to gather at The Chatel bar (commonly known as "Chet's") for afterwork drinks. I will leave it up to the reader to imagine the scenarios that resulted from excess alcohol and willing partners game for a "hookup." Unfortunately, these events that happened late at night were subsequently fodder for the gossip mill at work.

The "no fraternization" policy seemed to be abandoned outside of work hours, and lives, relationships, and reputations all suffered from the frequent "just one drink" promises that many of Grants' employees made to themselves and significant others.

The lessons I learned as a high school student in the part-time labor force were that:

1) If you want something, it is far more satisfying to earn it than to be dependent on the whims of those who have the money and the power to exploit you.

2) The workplace is a microcosm of society. Relationships, both good and bad, occur. Unfair treatment occurs.

3) Following the rules causes less trouble than breaking them.

4) If you don't like your status or your job, change it through education, diligence, and purpose-filled goals.

5) If you love your job, you will never have to work a day in your life.

Deirdre, Colleen, Maura, and I worked together frequently and often commuted together as well. Initially we would reject the invitations of older male and female employees to join them at Chet's for a drink after work. Instead, we would go to Friendly's across the street from the bar. As time went on, we saw more and more of our co-workers going into Chet's after Grants closed at nine. As curious and daring adolescent females, egging each other on, we eventually abandoned Friendly's for Chet's. We were all underage, but drinks would be thrust into our hands by older workers the moment we entered Chet's.

Adolescent stupidity prevented us from turning down free drinks or driving after consuming a beer or two. And worse, I have hated beer since I had my first, but if someone put one into my hand for free, I would sip it until I could see the bottom of the glass. To complicate matters even further, Deirdre's father was a Weymouth police officer whose family lived less than two miles from Chet's. I now consider dumb luck to be the only factor between our underage drinking and subsequent driving under the influence of alcohol that prevented any of us from being caught in our illegal behavior.

By this time, all four of us had our driver's licenses and started wandering farther and farther afield together when we had time off. Two of us had saved enough from working many hours to purchase our own used cars. That was another very useful lesson we learned while working at Grants. None of the four of us were given money by our parents. Aside from housing and the other obligations of parents to their nearly adult children, the four of us were responsible for our own clothing; further education; gas, insurance, and maintenance on our cars; and any other extraneous expenses. If we wanted to go away together for a weekend, the travel and entertainment costs were up to us.

Since these were common ethics of the working-class communities to which we all belonged, we never felt these to be unduly burdensome parental expectations. The three of us who went to college right after high school attended Massachusetts state colleges. Along with this came increasing amounts of freedom, much of it examples justifying "idle hands are the devil's workshop." If we weren't working or in school, we had a number of adventures and experiences that we later regretted.

Although the repercussions of two of these events were far different in my life, they were both memorable.

10

❦

Opportunity and Rejection

L ike many of the other college-bound students in my school, by eleventh grade I was immersed in investigating universities for my post-high-school education. One morning, I got a notification from my guidance counselor that she wished to see me during my 11 a.m. study period. I always got nervous when I was summoned to the guidance office, even though I should have expected that it might be related to the college search process.

Ms. Hoffman greeted me warmly and said, "I have some good news for you. Princeton University has invited the top two eleventh graders from high schools across the country to visit Princeton for a weekend this fall. You are one of the students invited."

She went on to explain that high school students selected would be bused to Princeton, housed with same-sex Princeton students, attend orientation sessions and a Princeton University football game (Go Tigers!), and also oriented to the lifetime of advantages forthcoming for Princeton University graduates. I was given permission by my parents to attend this prestigious event as long as I could get coverage for my part-time bakery shifts.

I did so. I had a breathtaking weekend full of excitement, anticipation, and glorious visions for my future at Princeton. The trip was further enhanced for me because when I first stepped on the bus that was to convey us to New Jersey, I noticed the seats were disproportionately filled with boys. Of 42 students from Massachusetts selected for this weekend at Princeton, only eight were female. As a young feminist, I was initially discouraged by the disparity in gender representation. However, it soon came to my attention that a group of 10 of these male students were from Boston Latin School.

I excitedly made my way through the throng on the bus and introduced myself to the BLS group as a former Girls' Latin student. Immediately they cleared a seat for me to sit among them. Other than the events that were sex-segregated (such as spending the nights in a Princeton dorm), I spent my time with the BLS boys. I had the time of my life!

The short story is that upon conclusion of the trip to Princeton, I dated one of the Boston Latin School boys for a few months. Time, distance, and differing interests other than academic came between us, and we stopped seeing each other.

At the start of the orientation weekend, I was assigned a Princeton admissions counselor who followed my personal and academic journey for the next 18 months. He expressed dismay that I worked 20 to 30 hours per week and suggested instead that I immerse myself fully in all things academic and extracurricular. He warned me that it was critical, as a potential Ivy League student, that my resume contain superlative standardized test scores, academic and athletic awards, a documented history of countless hours of community service, and evidence of leadership in as many spheres as possible. When I reminded him that I worked at various part-time jobs when I was not engaged in academic activities, he told me that my level of participation in the paid labor force would be a detriment to my likelihood of acceptance at Princeton.

But one never knows what the future holds. Decades later, I earned both a master's degree and a doctor of philosophy from another Ivy League school, Brown University. I had my Ivy League status while having been an integral part of the part-time and full-time labor force since age 14.

Kudos to Mrs. Driscoll and Ms. Hoffman for giving me the confidence during my years in the Weymouth schools to be a high achiever, despite what anyone else had predicted.

An essential characteristic of Boston's Boys' and Girls' Latin schools was that they were extremely academically challenging "exam" schools that relied on their students to be able to succeed in a high-pressure environment. Students were selected for attendance to the Latin schools on two criteria: residence in Boston and passing the extremely rigorous entrance exam. Thus, my academic records prior to coming to South Weymouth from Girls' Latin indicated that I was a potential Princeton University scholar.

My memories of my time spent at Boys' Latin School for summer courses between seventh and eighth grade were blissful. The boys with whom Girls' Latin students affiliated in classes and in our free time were smart, funny, and motivated to succeed. So, when I climbed on the bus taking our select group for the weekend at Princeton, I immediately greeted the Latin School boys who were seated together, telling them that I had gone to Girls' Latin for seventh and eighth grade. Once I had passed along that information, the BLS kids and I became instant friends, and for the first time in my life, I had a coterie of boys surrounding me for the weekend.

However, the girls on the trip were informally chaperoned by female Princeton undergraduates, and the boys became weekend younger brothers to male Princetonians. We were only really chaperoned in the evenings and nights, as we were all assigned same-sex Princeton roommates. During the days, we were given tours around campus and attended lectures. Since I was the only former Latin School Girl, the Latin School boys stayed around me the entire weekend. I have never before, nor since, been so popular.

By the end of the weekend, I had paired off with Gordon, and we rode home together side by side, surrounded by the other Latin School boys teasing and harassing us. Forget Princeton, I wanted to finish high school at Boys Latin!

Gordon and I began long-distance dating, as he lived in Roslindale in the city of Boston. He had his own car, and after numerous nighttime phone calls—which increased in length each night (to the height of a five-hour, middle-of-the-night phone call, since I had my own room, and my own phone, and my own phone bill)—Gordon and I made plans for him to come to South Weymouth, pick me up, and take me to a movie at Westgate Mall in Brockton.

I was driving at the time as well, but I have never had a good sense of direction. As I write this story decades later, my sense of direction has not improved, and I am not at ease with electronics, including the GPS in my car. Suffice it to say, I have always been somewhat or completely lost wherever I have been heading.

Gordon picked me up at my family home, and my mother, who was usually very timid, was rather effusive that I was now officially dating a high-achieving Jewish student from Boston Latin School.

By the way, my mother's earlier rejection of non-Catholics did not extend to the Jewish people. Since she herself had grown up in a Jewish neighborhood in Dorchester, she had great admiration for successful Jewish men who, as she had observed, "were very good to their wives."

Gordon pulled up to the house and came in to say hello to my parents. My mother seemed delighted to see him and wished us a pleasant night at the movies. We set off in his car up toward Columbian Square, passing through till we reached Route 18. We took a left to head to Westgate Mall in Brockton, with me guiding him through South Shore cities and towns in which he had never been.

I had been to Westgate Mall many times before, but usually with my friends, who had been driving a year longer than I had. I hadn't ever really had to pay attention to the specific route to the mall. At one point I told Gordon that he should take the next right, a main road. As we traveled for a couple of miles, the sites looked unfamiliar even to me. I hemmed and hawed before I said, "Umm, Gordon, I gave you the wrong directions. I think we should have taken the next major right turn."

To my shock, Gordon raised his voice and screamed at me. He shouted, "*You're the one who lives around here! How could you get us lost?*" He waved his arms around and glared at me for a moment. It was enough to make my blood run hot with anger. Quietly I said to him, "Gordon, take me home." He ignored me and kept driving. He hadn't gone a quarter of a mile farther when I said more insistently, "I asked you to take me home. Please turn the car around now." Gordon looked at me in shock.

"Judy," he beseeched me, "you've got to be kidding. We're going to the movies. Are you mad at me?"

I quietly answered, "Gordon, you screamed at me. Nobody is allowed to raise their voice at me like you just did. Take me home."

My father had been a screamer and a hitter, and I had seen enough additional domestic violence in my life, in numerous families, that I had already determined I would never tolerate anyone berating me in any way, especially in a threatening way such as screaming at me.

Gordon lowered his voice and softly said to me, "Judy, I am sorry. Please forgive me. Let's just forget that I yelled at you and go to the movies."

Stonily, I said, "I asked you to please take me home. Are you going to do it, or do I have to get out of the car while you are driving?"

Gordon began to apologize profusely to me. Yet I was immovable in my resolve to end this date. I managed to direct him back to my house correctly, and he pulled up, shut the car off, and turned toward me. I said "goodbye" firmly but politely and got out of the car, immediately going into the house.

My mother was shocked to see me and asked why I was home. I answered simply that he had screamed at me in the car for having told him the wrong direction. She looked perplexed.

It was difficult to have listened to my father's angry shouting much of my life, but I knew that I would never be in a relationship with someone who raised their voice at me. My father was, at the time, still a shouter who went from happy to enraged in a heartbeat.

I went up to my room and lay on the bed, replaying the scene over and over in my head. Each time I knew that I had done what was right for me.

Gordon called me steadily for a couple of weeks. I asked him to stop calling. He then called me on random occasions for the next few months. I began to doubt my decision, wondering why I would have given up such a smart and success-oriented boyfriend, who was definitely infatuated with me and whom I really liked, "just" for raising his voice. For months following the Princeton weekend, but before we actually went out for a date, we had shared so many hours of the day and evening on the phone. One night, we had conversed both playfully and seriously from 10 p.m. to 3 a.m., talking about our future, telling each other funny stories, and essentially enjoying each other's company. Remembering these enjoyable conversations, I began to regret my decision to end the relationship. However, I replayed in my head his sudden angry screams directed at me for a minor error on my part. I steeled myself to not give in and call him.

For the readers of this story, my reaction may seem overly dramatic. I have no idea how Gordon's life progressed after that night. I hope that he learned that screaming is not an acceptable way to communicate with people about whom you care. Screaming indicates uncontrolled anger and might well be used by the person on the receiving end to infer that the fury expressed verbally may result in physical attacks. At the very least, screaming diminishes the importance of the person with whom the screamer is communicating, and, in my estimation, is an indicator of the potential for violence.

I took a chance. I dated a young man with a great deal of potential. We had similar goals, we enjoyed a lot of the same activities, and I thought that we had shared values. That might all have been true, despite what he demonstrated to me by screaming at me. Maybe. Maybe not. I never gave him the opportunity to direct violence at me again.

And by the way, my application to Princeton was also rejected. As a part of the grooming process for Ivy League candidates, each applicant with significant potential for admission is assigned an admissions process counselor. The counselor meets with the candidate in person and requests numerous academic, athletic, and other endorsements and recommendations from graduates of the Ivy League institution to which the candidate has applied. A significant component of the application process is a weekly phone call with the assigned admissions advisor. I provided all the information requested, and my application was immediately flagged. My admissions counselor telephoned me and stated that he was stunned to find that I was employed an average of 25 hours per week, thus limiting the time that I had available for extracurricular activities and community service. I confirmed what he had to say, offering no apologies or excuses. He answered that it was extremely unlikely that I would be accepted. I did not make any appeals or apologies.

I got to the Ivy League eventually. It was far more satisfying to graduate from Brown University with a PhD in Sociology at age 45 than it would have been to be accepted to Princeton at age 17 with specific demands on how I should live my life to be considered to be an acceptable candidate.

I sincerely hope that Gordon stopped yelling at women.

11

❦

Saint Patrick's Day in South Boston

South Boston is a densely populated neighborhood of Boston located south and east of the Fort Point Channel and abutting Dorchester Bay. Commonly called "Southie," South Boston has undergone a number of demographic changes since becoming part of the city of Boston in 1804. This section of Boston is popularly known by its twentieth-century identity as a working-class Irish Catholic community. South Boston has left its mark on the history of Boston busing desegregation, but it is also home to the St. Patrick's Day parade. March 17 is St. Patrick's Day all over the world, but Boston's St. Patrick's Day parade is a celebration both of Irish-American culture and the Evacuation Day observance of the British leaving Boston during the American Revolutionary War on March 17, 1776.

Bostonians were the first to celebrate St. Patrick's Day in North America. The St. Patrick's Day parade is celebrated on the Sunday closest to March 17. The parade and subsequent parties attract thousands upon thousands of participants. If one can find a space to stand, anyone can attend the parade. Thousands mill around the streets of Boston, enjoying the party atmosphere until it is finally over. However, limited parking in South Boston is a considerable barrier to many who want to come into Southie to be physically present for the parade. The often-ubiquitous alcoholic drinks enjoyed by thousands of attendees at the St. Patrick's Day Parade are deemed legal if consumed indoors. Thus, having family or friends with a home in Southie, especially along the parade route, is the golden ticket to enjoying the parade, particularly for those who like their Guinness!

Luckily (or not) for me, Colleen, and Maura, Deirdre had a cousin who lived directly on the parade route on Broadway. The parade begins at the Broadway transit station, then continues along Broadway through most of South Boston. The route bends slightly at the change from West Broadway to East Broadway at the intersection of Dorchester Street. It finishes at Farragut Road.

We were invited to what was to be a small family gathering in the relative's second-floor apartment. All of the attendees for the parade gathered outside in crowds three to four people deep to see the entirety of the parade. Since we had a place to be inside, all the invited friends and relatives congregated in a roomy three-bedroom apartment with celebrants of all ages. I was introduced to Deirdre's cousins, who occupied the Broadway apartment, but the crowd got larger and larger as the day wore on.

Since I had driven the four of us friends to the party, I was increasingly concerned about leaving my car on the street, or worse, driving home from South Boston to South Weymouth with a large number of presumably intoxicated drivers on the road.

I made it clear to my three friends that I was not staying long after the parade ended. However, they had already begun to celebrate before the parade began, grabbing the plentiful bottles and cans of beer and other intoxicating liquids and downing them rapidly. I was drinking only nonalcoholic beverages. I started to get anxious, perceiving that the party was getting more and more out of hand quickly once the parade had passed our viewing area on a small section of Broadway.

Unfortunately, I had no way of predicting that Ed, the husband of the hostess, would take a shine to me. My friends and I were dressed appropriately for the parade party in bell-bottom pants with block-heeled shoes and miniskirts with green blouses and black go-go boots. Virtually all the grown-ups were drinking alcohol, and most were smoking. The women, as was typical for the time, clustered in the kitchen and fed their kids any manner of food naturally or artificially green for the day. I stayed close to my friends in the mobbed apartment. My friend Colleen noticed Ed's attentive eyes on me and said, "Watch out, you've got an admirer." I was more worried than flattered. The crowd was getting a bit out of control. I asked her, "Who is it?" She responded, "It's Ed, the husband of that woman right over there. It's their apartment." He saw us looking his way and came right over. Ed immediately asked me if I wanted a tour of the neighborhood. I grabbed Dierdre's hand and demanded, "Don't you leave me even for a minute! I just came for the parade!" I saw Ed's wife glaring in my direction, so I politely declined his invitation and dashed outside, dragging Dierdre and friends with me.

I was honestly scared. Ed followed us outside and stood in front of the triple-decker where my friends and I had gathered as we started making plans to go home. I had driven everyone in my car to the parade, and I was leaving now because of my discomfort. But then Deirdre, Colleen, and Maura wandered off into the street parties, which were standard protocol following the Saint Patrick's Day parades.

I was alone and Ed again asked if I wanted to go for a walk. His wife's glaring at me in the house had shaken me far more than his presence with me now. I was adamant in telling him that I was leaving. I looked in my pocketbook, but the keys weren't there. I recalled that I had a light jacket on when we had arrived, and I had apparently left the garment inside the apartment with the keys in the pocket. I was now extremely uncomfortable and more than a little bit scared of Ed's wife, but I couldn't leave without retrieving the keys and those were inside, as was she.

Finally, Ed was convinced I was uninterested in hanging out with him and left me alone. I crept up the backstairs to the second floor, hoping to find the jacket on the arm of a chair. But the crowd in the apartment was almost impenetrable. I tried to slip in unnoticed by the angry wife, who believed me to be after her husband. If anything, I had ditched him outside. The last thing in the world that I wanted was someone's husband! Suddenly, I saw the wife (a bit tipsy by now, as were most of the people at the party). She was looking in my direction but appeared not to have seen me. I slid in between the refrigerator and the stove, half crouching, until I could make my way into the living room and search again for my misplaced apparel.

Suddenly, I heard Ed's wife scream, "Grab that stringy mop

beside the refrigerator!" Sure she meant me, especially because of my long and now unkempt hair, I ran out into the living room, grabbed my jacket and keys, and jumped down the back steps two at a time. I was glad to hear my friends running down the stairs behind me, but they were all laughing hysterically. I was furious!

They had seen the quick event in the kitchen, saw me white-faced with fear and now fleeing the scene! They got to the car right after I did, and I demanded to know "What was so funny?" I suspected that one of them, as a prank, had told the husband where I was hiding and that had angered the wife, directing anyone close by to seize me!

I yelled at them, *"Didn't you hear her say to someone to grab that stringy mop by the refrigerator?* She wanted to beat me up!" My three supposed friends were nearly rolling on the ground with uncontrollable laughter. Gasping for breath, Deirdre said, "She wanted the actual *mop.* One of the kids had just dropped a whole bottle of Coke on the floor. Nobody else but us saw you grab your jacket and run from the apartment!"

By now I was furious at all of them. I protested, "That wife wanted to kill me, and I didn't do anything." I had tears streaming down my reddened cheeks as I was truly afraid and embarrassed. I told my friends that if they didn't stop laughing, they could all find another way home as I was not going to let them in my car.

Not knowing how they would get home to South Weymouth from South Boston on Saint Patrick's Day, they apologized, but I could hear them snickering all the way home. I never told them the rest of the story because I was still so angry at them. The husband did pursue me briefly after that. He asked another work friend who was also at the party for my personal phone number. Unaware of the events of the afternoon, the work friend gave him my number. With earnings from my jobs, I had bought both my own car and my own blue, princess-style telephone. I was shocked and scared when he called me at home, and he was perceptive enough to hear it in my voice. He reassured me that his intent was just to get to know me and be my friend. I politely but clearly said *"No"* and asked him not to call me again. It took one more call to convince him that the Saint Patrick's Day party had been disturbing both to his wife and to me, and that if there were any more calls, I would have my phone disconnected. He apologized to me and that was the end of the story. Except for the times when one of my friends would randomly yell out, "*Somebody grab that stringy mop by the refrigerator.*" I'd remind them with a glare that their joke was unacceptable! I've never attended another St. Patrick's Day party in my life. Instead, I stay home and play my own collection of Irish music. Sometimes I slip in between my own refrigerator and the kitchen wall just for old times' sake.

12

ↂ

Inspired by the Women's Movement

From the time I was in junior high, no matter which school I was attending, I was enrolled in college preparatory programs. We were encouraged early on to search out colleges which would be compatible with our interests, abilities, and life goals. I always knew that I would go to college. What I didn't know was that my father didn't necessarily have the same plan for his daughters.

Throughout the precollege years, I spent much of my time in junior high and high school guidance offices perusing the hundreds of college catalogs and wondering which one I would ultimately attend. I would fantasize about what dorm living would be like and wonder which state I would live in while attending college. I decided by age 16 that I "definitely" wanted to attend law school. My father was mixed in his messages to me about his true feelings about my intended vocation. I found out many years later that my father had often told my mother that "college was a waste of time for girls because they just got married and had kids anyway." My mother never said much about college to us. My mother always chose her battles with my father. In her silent plan, her daughters as well as her sons *would* go to college, and it would be with her emotional support, but on our own dimes.

My father was a very ambitious man, busy building his career. Over the period of time in which he married my mother until they had children from tots to teens at the same time, my father's primary spheres were his job and his education. My mother's primary sphere was the home and the kids. This was absolutely consistent with the times, although the second wave of the women's movement in the 1960s and 1970s started having a critical effect on females throughout the US and the rest of the developed world.

My mother, like most "housewives," married my father right after they both graduated from high school. Between the ages of 19 and 36 they had seven children. My mother bore a full load of housekeeping and childcare and took evening classes at Northeastern University when she could. Husbands, at the time, were considered to be the "head of the family." Women were subject to their husband's decisions in most matters. If women worked outside of the home out of necessity or choice, their jobs were limited to a few professions. The 38 percent of American women who worked outside their homes in the 1960s were largely confined to jobs as teachers, nurses, or secretaries. Working women were routinely paid lower salaries than men and denied opportunities for advancement in the workplace. Employers assumed that working women, particularly those who had children, would soon become pregnant again and quit their jobs. Women also were offered lower wages, as it was assumed that husbands and fathers, "heads of household," deserved higher wages because they had families to support.

In 1962, Betty Friedan published the groundbreaking book *The Feminine Mystique*, in which she captured the frustration and despair of a generation of college-educated housewives who felt trapped and unfulfilled. She called upon both educated and uneducated women to seek their own fulfillment in work outside the home. Friedan's work was credited with sparking the second wave of the American feminist movement. Decades earlier, the woman's suffrage movement, or first wave, culminated in the passage of the Nineteenth Amendment, which gave women the right to vote in 1920. Influenced strongly by Friedan's work, a new generation of women would seek equality beyond the law and into their lives.

The feminist movement of the 1960s and 1970s focused on dismantling workplace inequality and making gender discrimination illegal. When the newly established Equal Employment Opportunity Commission would not enforce the law's protection of women workers, a group of feminists took action. Along with Betty Friedan, the National Organization for Women (NOW) was founded to lobby Congress for gender equality laws and to assist women in their court battles against gender discrimination in the workplace.

My father, in particular, did not realize that his daughters were being enlightened by the women's rights movement. He was still very much of the mind that women should be subject to men, and that men were superior to women in all aspects of life. When I was old enough to drive, I visited my father at his job after he had just received a significant promotion and raise in pay. He invited me in to see his roomy office in the executive area of the building, and he summoned in his secretary. He introduced me to one of his male colleagues and casually asked us if we wanted tea or coffee. I noticed the secretary jotting down my father's instructions for the hot beverages, and I became unsettled. My father paused, looked at me, and demanded, "Tell Betty what you'd like." I was furious! I looked at Betty and said, "Let me come with you and get the tea and coffee and I'll bring it back here." My father became enraged, and quickly said, "No, Betty. Go ahead. We're all set." I looked back at my father, mirroring his own florid face. He yelled at me in front of his male colleague, "*What did you just do? Why were you so rude?*" I gritted my teeth and answered my father, "Surely, Betty has other work to do than to wait on us." He exploded at me, "That *is* her job!" As my father had had heart disease from a young age, I decided to let it go before I had to perform CPR on him in his own office. I politely excused myself and left. As I got outside his office, I heard my father apologize to his male colleague for my "ignorant behavior."

I was just starting to enjoy all of the opportunities that I believed would be wide open to me in the future. I quickly realized that if I were counting on my father to support my educational and career goals, I needed to change my plans. Fortunately, I had always had female guidance counselors, and many female teachers were coming along in this road to women's equality along with me. Students, both male and female, were being educated about the roles of women and men in society. The messages were being reinforced that women needed to push and to be willing to be perceived as difficult (at best), if there was to be a new perception of the roles open to women.

We paid attention to the goals and the plans of the National Organization for Women, and we also learned from the more radical "women's liberation movement," whose plan was to overthrow the patriarchy regarding their roles in every facet of women's lives. The women's liberation movement popularized the idea that "the personal is political"—that women's political equality had equally important personal ramifications.

I started to look to my mother for more support regarding my future plans. She was following the fight for women's equality closely, but she was just at the beginning stages of her transformation of perceiving herself to be living in a male-centered society, one that could be changed into an equal rights-centered society. With five daughters and two sons, my mother was getting pressure from the older girls to make a better life for herself, and to raise the little daughters with the confidence to expect equality with men in our country.

So, the battleground over colleges for me was a silent one. My mother never told me, but she had unilaterally decided that Kathy (the oldest) and I would go to Bridgewater State College, to which we could both commute by car. We would be able to keep our part-time jobs close to home, and weekly pay from our part-time jobs would finance our education. Kathy followed my mother's preordained plan exactly. I started off as my mother had intended, and then as my own wants and needs changed, I made numerous poor choices but ultimately succeeded at my long-term goals (albeit the hard way).

Without knowing my mother's plan for my life, I applied to and was accepted to some of the private colleges of my choice. But then I learned my parents had informed these colleges that I would be turning down their acceptances if they were contingent on my parents paying my bills.

I did not send in an application to Bridgewater State College. Instead, my parents filled it out and sent it in without my knowledge. My acceptance came and they did send money to BSC—just the nominal fee to hold my place for Fall 1972 admission. I was enraged, but at that point, I couldn't do anything about it. I finally became determined that despite my resentment about the way my attendance at Bridgewater State came about, I would make my own path.

13

⚜

Entering Bridgewater

My first day at Bridgewater State College was memorable in a happy way. The commute was convenient, the drive took only about a half-hour, and there was a brand-new freshman parking lot available.

The first two buildings I encountered were the Science Building, which also housed the Kelly Gymnasium and an Olympic-size swimming pool, and, across the street, the Maxwell Library. The library came to be one of my two favorite buildings on the entire campus. Equally as important to the students was the Student Union Building, which housed the large, round cafeteria with a circular wall of windows, making it a bright and airy retreat for the primarily commuter students every day.

On the first day of classes, all the first-year male and female students were ushered into the auditorium for our orientation. We were directed to take our designated seats, which were arranged alphabetically. I had no idea how much impact this placement would have on me to this day. While waiting for academic presentations to begin, most of us sat uncomfortably with our lack of knowledge of what to expect of today, next week, or our entire college careers. The vast majority of us were to use our campus maps for the next month or so to find our way around, but we wanted to feel settled in as quickly as possible.

How to do that? Find friends immediately! Given my last name was Kirwan, I was seated between Donna Keefe and Alice

Kornan. I looked to my left and saw Alice, a pretty young woman with waist-length brown hair, who looked like she felt as uncomfortable as I did. But she had a friendly smile. As Donna looked to her immediate right to assess the friendship candidacy of the new student next to her, I looked to my left and saw poor Alice—a quivering mess. I felt the same inside as Alice did, but I didn't perceive her as someone with whom I could share my jumbled emotions at the time. I turned back to Donna on my right. I noticed that Donna had quickly turned from the person on her right and then back to me. We laughed nervously and said, "Well, I guess you are my new friend." At least our assessment skills were acute: Donna has been one of my closest friends for over 50 years.

We immediately were joined at the hip, especially since we were both elementary education majors. But then a scary moment happened that put us back in our uncomfortable places. A few raps of the gavel indicated that faculty presentations were beginning. An official of the college greeted us solemnly and said, "Look to the left of you, and look to the right of you. One of you will be gone by the end of the first year at Bridgewater State College."

I wondered where we would be going, and which of us it would be. It was not the most encouraging way to begin our freshman year, especially since he was warning us that the rigid curricular standards would weed us out if we did not take our college program seriously. Donna and I moved a little closer to each other in our seats and practically were holding hands for comfort as we left the auditorium after the conclusion of the scare tactics.

But it didn't get better that day. We had each been given our predetermined first semester freshman schedules. Following the orientation, we were sent on our way to the first class of our college careers. Donna and I saw that we had identical schedules. That gave the two of us, who had not even met two hours previously, great comfort. We checked our maps to find out where our Western Civilization class would be held. We found our way to the correct building and took seats next to each other. As the classroom filled with students looking as bewildered as we felt, we noticed that there was no professor at the front of the room. We all sat and squirmed uncomfortably. When the class became quiet, in strode a fearful-looking man, a twin to Colonel Klink from *Hogan's Heroes*. That popular situation comedy of the era was set in a Nazi prisoner-of-war camp during World War II. Colonel Wilhelm Klink was the monocle-wearing commandant of the camp. Both Professor Wolf, our first teacher in college, and Colonel Klink were frightful individuals.

Professor Wolf took his place at the front of the class as we all twitched in our seats, not knowing what to expect. We did hope for a warm, welcoming speech from the esteemed professor, but he did not look as if smiling was in his plan for the day. He looked silently around the room, row by row and seat by seat, intimidating each of us into complete stillness.

After a pause of a couple of minutes, he commanded us to *"Take out your notebooks and pens."* We looked from him to each other, and to other students in the room for their reactions to his dictum. Was he joking? Were we supposed to laugh? When he restated his demand, a little bit louder now, we knew he meant business. But it was the first day! Weren't we just here to find out about the course and what our expectations were to be?

A moment later, he roared, *"Get out! Get out, all of you!* I expected college students to be prepared to take notes from the first day forward! I don't see textbooks. I don't see that any of you are ready to be college students! *Get out and don't come back until you are ready to behave like college students!"*

We left the room, a number of male and female students in tears, the rest of us trembling, at the very least. Maybe today was the day to make that prediction come true that one out of three of us would not be here at the end of the school year. Worse, I might not be here at the end of the first day! But I don't scare easily, and I did go back prepared, along with Donna, the next day. I have no idea how many students dropped the required class, or even their college career, that day.

And it still was not over. We had a few more classes that first day, and they happily turned out to be what we expected of introductory sessions. Finally, our last class scheduled for the day was gym, or, in our case, Freshman Swim.

Donna and I entered the swimming pool locker room with both male and female students. That was another unpleasant shock. We fortunately were diverted into sex-specific dressing rooms, but then two matrons started yelling at the female group of students as we wandered in. *"What's your bra size?"* they demanded to know!

I instinctively crossed my arms over my chest and got red in the face. Donna and I looked at each other, temporarily stunned, until they screamed at us again, "*What's your bra size?*" I stammered "34 B," and the woman threw a one-piece, braless swimsuit at me and demanded that I get a locker, get my swimsuit with swim cap provided on, and get into the pool immediately, as our instructor was waiting.

We girls huddled together in a mass against the walls around the pool, nearly crying when we saw the freshman boys coming in through another door, also in swimsuits. *What? Co-ed* swimming? I hadn't signed up for this. In fact, nobody had. We were not allowed to opt out of any classes to which we had been assigned. Well, forcing us to get into swimsuits in mixed company resulted in a mass dive of new students into the chilly Olympic-size pool.

"What could be worse than this?" I whimpered to Donna. Yes, in this whole day, this was the most unbearable part to me. Donna shrugged as she shivered. And then I realized what would be worse. The class ran the entire semester, so by the end of the course (which would not end till mid-December), we would be leaving the frigid pool with cold bodies and wet hair for even colder temperatures outside. I decided to convince Donna to take folk dancing with me for our second semester of the gym requirement.

BSC was considered to be the most conservative of the state colleges and universities, compared for example with the University of Massachusetts at Amherst (also known as "Zoo Mass"). Despite its very conventional reputation, we were the first in the state system, in 1973, to have what was called a "streaker." "Streaking" was a popular act at the time, running stark naked through a public area as a prank or on a dare. In the wintertime, streakers were often seen wearing wool hats in addition only to footwear.

I couldn't believe it when it happened! My friends and I were sitting in the cafeteria when a naked man came running through that much-used, on-campus gathering spot. Everyone laughed and campus police were summoned. The streaker wasn't caught. When I got home that evening, I watched the Boston news broadcast, and Bridgewater State College was the opening story with this very atypical event for the institution.

Back for a moment to the scare tactics of our freshman orientation lecture earlier that morning. They had predicted that one of us would be gone by the end of the first year. It was Donna. She applied on a whim for an unspecified government job in Washington, DC. The review of her qualifications, checking of recommendations, and background checks alone took nine full months. But Donna was one of very few applicants who made it through the grueling process. By the next fall, she was happily employed in the nation's capital and living in Virginia.

I stayed for two years at Bridgewater State College and grew to love it. But as my interests changed from education to health sciences, I found that Bridgewater did not have the range of courses I needed. At that point, I left Bridgewater and transferred to Boston State College.

Another factor motivated my transfer, however. Even as a small child, one of my primary objectives was pleasing my mother. If she wanted something, I found a way to get it for her. When I was close to completing my second year of undergraduate education at Bridgewater State College, I stopped at my parent's home in South Weymouth for a visit and a cup of tea with my mother one fateful day.

After we finished the tea and a benign chat, she said she had to take her laundry into her first-floor bedroom. After more time elapsed than was necessary for her to put her clean clothing away, I called to her. She answered, but her voice sounded a bit odd to me. I went down the short hallway and found that her bedroom door was partly closed.

"Mum," I called, "are you alright? Can I come in?" She answered, "I am okay. Come on in." My mother was rearranging clothing in her closet with her back to me. I asked again, "Mum, are you okay?" She answered, "I'm feeling a little sad."

Perplexed, I continued, "Can you tell me what's wrong?" My mother turned to me and somewhat mournfully said, "I have five daughters and not one of you is a nurse!" My immediate response was, "I'll do it! I'll go to nursing school for you!"

It seems strange even to me that I would answer her in that way because it was never in my life plan to become a registered nurse! However, as described in chapter 21 of my first book, *Dorchester Girl,* aptly called "The Enabler," I had compulsively acceded to most of her wishes all of her life—with the exception of me getting married at age 18! Likely still feeling guilty that I had upset her two years previously with my early marriage, I thought that I had made up for this egregious error by continuing to work numerous hours a week while endeavoring to complete my college education.

I immediately started to research nursing schools. I found that Boston State College was about to start a baccalaureate program in nursing. This was not a degree available at Bridgewater.

I closely examined the science curriculum at Bridgewater and found there were not enough health science courses available that might be transferrable to a college that did have a nursing degree if I decided to stay at Bridgewater and then transfer. There was no major at Bridgewater that would even be close to nursing except speech pathology, but that was not what my mother wanted.

I reviewed other schools and started to consider transferring to Boston State College on Huntington Avenue. By this time, I had completed half of my college career at Bridgewater and was very comfortable there. But it was clear that I could not meet my new objectives if I didn't make a change.

Boston State College *was* in the process of developing a bachelor's degree in nursing, but it was just in the preliminary phases of developing a curriculum and accepting its first students. Yet it had a large slate of nursing-appropriate courses in both natural science and biology. I made the appointment for an interview at Boston State College with the objective of investigating the possibility of transferring there in the fall of 1974.

I was very conflicted: I loved Bridgewater State College; I was on track to graduate in two more years; and it was possible that completing a nursing program that was just getting off the ground would delay my graduation. I was hesitant, yet the thought that my mother *wanted* me to be a nurse was very compelling to me. I decided to take a chance on Boston State College, hoping fervently to graduate with an RN degree in 1976.

This rather extreme compulsion to please my mother at least most of the time had shaped my life since early childhood. My early marriage was the major exception. She was definitely not pleased by that but ultimately accepted it as long as I completed my college education. Now there was this new expectation that I would honor my promise to become an RN for my mother. I hoped that I was doing the right thing for myself as well.

I went to my interview at Boston State, and by the end of the meeting with an admissions counselor, I indeed found myself enrolled for fall of 1974. I was able to transfer two full years of college credits from Bridgewater State College to Boston State College; it seemed possible that I could still graduate as planned in 1976, but the actual college major that I could complete by that time was unknown.

The fly in the ointment was that the newly forming baccalaureate program in registered nursing was slow in getting off the ground. Within months of my transfer from Bridgewater State College to Boston State College, it became crystal clear to me that it was highly unlikely that Boston State's planned nursing program would be fully operational any time soon. Friends who had been accepted into the anticipated program were soon informed that they would *not* be graduating from a National League for Nursing-certified program at Boston State until at least 1977, if not later.

I panicked. I could not possibly keep extending my time in school without a guaranteed graduation date. I decided to change my major to natural sciences with a minor in biology and meet my original expectations of receiving my bachelor's degree by May of 1976. In September of 1976 I would then attend Newton-Wellesley Hospital School of Nursing for a two-year registered nurse diploma program. Upon graduation in 1978, I would be eligible to take the Massachusetts State Board of Registration exam in nursing.

The transfer from Bridgewater to Boston State was an adjustment in many ways, both good and bad. Major changes such as this are always difficult. The commute would be a challenge from Braintree, since I did not have my own car. However, it happened that I was able to take a bus, a train, and then a trolley, starting across the street from my apartment in Braintree and ending at the front door of Boston State College on Huntington Avenue. I was ecstatic to be back in Boston, the place of my birth!

14

⁓

Back in the City of Boston

O ne situation for which I was unprepared when I abruptly
transferred to Boston State College from bucolic Bridgewater State College was that city life is often dramatically
different from suburban life. I was now, for many hours a day, back
in the city of Boston, where mandatory school desegregation by
means of forced busing was just about to begin.

The busing plan formulated by Judge Arthur Garrity had
come about because the schools in Boston were determined to be
racially separate and unequal. Black children were denied access to
many programs, services, and school supplies available to children
in primarily white schools. The Garrity plan called for forced in-
tegration of South Boston High School and Roxbury High School.
South Boston High School students were largely white and of Irish
parentage. The majority of students at Roxbury High School were
black. The plan had been fought in the courts for years. It was not
wanted by blacks or whites, and racism and violence increased in
the city of Boston both during consideration and implementation
of the plan. Violence was rampant.

A daily exchange of students by forced busing was to commence on September 12, 1974, my twentieth birthday and just
weeks into my first semester at Boston State College.

Boston State College had two campuses: the main campus on
Huntington Avenue, which bordered Mission Hill in Roxbury, and
the Fenway campus, which sat behind Fenway Park on Lansdowne
Street. Both were accessible to me by public transportation. The

Fenway Campus was a 15-minute walk or so from the Huntington Campus. Frequent rioting erupted throughout the city, but in particular in the Roxbury neighborhoods adjacent to the Huntington campus, and in South Boston.

Because of the radical opposition to forced busing that most residents of the city expressed, violence continued to increase. This was not a solution to the ever-present racism and inequality in the city of Boston. Many have, in retrospect, referred to the Garrity plan as the greatest failure of a social experiment in American history.

Even though Boston State College was not a high school, school buses were a primary target of people's rage about forced busing. The identity or age of the riders made no difference to those who threw rocks at the yellow school buses, tipped them over while they were carrying students, or even set them on fire (along with police cruisers monitoring the city streets).

We had been advised as Boston State students to take our assigned yellow buses to the Fenway campus from the Huntington campus and back to avoid being victims of interpersonal violence in the streets. However, if we rode the buses in either direction, we often had to ride with our heads resting on our laps to avoid the projectiles which were hurled at all yellow school buses. The violence was not limited to the bused high school students who were involuntary participants in this institutionalized violence.

An irony is that William Bratton, considered to be one of America's "top cops," was attending Boston State on the GI bill following his years of service in the military. The GI Bill, officially titled "The Servicemen's Readjustment Act of 1944," offered benefits to many former members of the military, including coverage of tuition and expenses while attending college or trade school. Bratton was among many students who were noticeable among the student body for their older and wiser countenances due to varying periods of military service.

Many years later, when I was teaching at Curry College in Milton, Massachusetts, Bratton presented a lecture on his years as head of local, national, and international law enforcement concerns. I attended Bratton's lecture with my class of 25 criminal justice students, who were also working police officers in cities and towns throughout the state. At the time, Curry was one of a number of colleges in Massachusetts that provided the Police Career Incentive

Pay Program (PCIPP) through the Quinn Bill, which was enacted by the Massachusetts legislature to encourage police officers to earn degrees in law enforcement and criminal justice.

The rest of Bratton's audience at Curry College was made up of students of all ages and others from the Boston area who were simply interested in hearing Bratton speak.

During his lecture, Bratton mentioned that he had attended Boston State College during mandatory school desegregation in Boston during the same years in which I attended Boston State. He commented wryly that during the day, he was a welcome member of many classes at BSC. However, when he donned his police riot gear, including a helmet with a face shield, for his afternoon shifts patrolling the violent streets of Boston, he was unrecognizable to students with whom he attended classes during the day. Bratton commented that some of these very classmates were the same people throwing rocks at him and his fellow officers as they attempted to maintain order amid the rioting in the streets surrounding the college which he attended.

Mandatory school desegregation through forced busing in Boston in the late 1970s through the early 1980s was doomed from the start. From the very first day that busing was instituted, the Boston police were outnumbered by violent protesters in the streets. The Massachusetts State Police were summoned the first day when it became obvious that the BPD alone could not contain the violence in South Boston, Roxbury, and throughout the city as a result of this widely reviled plan.

As a Boston State College student, I was not involved in the busing plan. However, resistance to busing was ubiquitous and violence could not be contained. Collateral damage was everywhere. If you were anywhere in the city during those tumultuous years, you were a potential victim of the potent hatred that was manifested toward police officers and ordinary citizens.

I graduated from Boston State College with a degree in natural science in 1976—on time and with a transcript that left me well prepared for my next step: attending Newton-Wellesley Hospital School of Nursing.

At graduation, my shy mother could be heard above the crowd screaming congratulations to me, since I was finally on my way to nursing school!

15

⁓

Marry in Haste, Repent at Leisure

My first marriage took place during my first year of college. Having since reflected on my own stupidity at that age too many times to count, I cannot just blame my impulsive decision to get married at age 18 on immaturity. I attribute much of my choice to the attention Wayne lavished on me, something that I was not used to receiving at home.

Additionally, as I learned in a graduate course, "Sociology of the Family," at Brown University, one of the most common reasons individuals pair up with other individuals is convenience. In trying to anticipate the answer to the question our graduate professor asked us about how we made decisions to date another person, most of us in the class assumed that likely predictors would include compatibility in numerous areas of life. We expected that education levels, career plans, and mutual agreement about where to establish a home together, as well as other such commonsense factors, would predict whom a person might date and with whom they might mate. Instead, experts in family studies from the 1990s concluded that convenience *alone* was the reason many people paired up, whether as friends or as couples. Unfortunately, I am a living example of that phenomenon.

However, couples do have the ability to uncouple! That saved my sanity.

As the second oldest in a large family, I had numerous

responsibilities for the care of our home and my five younger siblings. I started earning my own money at age eight and became enrolled in the formal work force at age 14. In other words, I was working, getting a paycheck, and paying taxes as a young teen.

It was while working at Grants evenings and Saturdays that I met Wayne, a young, full-time shoe salesman. I was assigned to the cosmetics department adjacent to the shoe department. I found it very attractive that Wayne was a Navy veteran, had his own two-bedroom apartment in nearby Braintree, and always drove the latest model sports cars. All of the superficial details of his life were immediately appealing to me.

Additionally, he showered me with gifts. That was something I could definitely appreciate. I was by then attending Bridgewater State College as a freshman student studying elementary education. He got annoyed with the amount of time I dedicated to homework, making me less available to go out in the evenings with him. I got home from college one afternoon, and my mother met me at the front door. She was clearly furious. I had no idea what I could have done to make her so angry. She demanded that I come with her up to my bedroom. Immediately she pointed to a brand-new desk that had been delivered to me from Kincaid's Furniture in Quincy. Her face purple with rage, she yelled at me, "He's giving you the rush!" I had no idea who "he" was or to where or how I was being rushed. I looked at her quizzically and she demanded between gritted teeth, "Why would someone buy you a gift like that?" I had no answer.

As angry as my mother was, I was speechless with delight. No one had ever given me a gift of that magnitude before. I no longer had to do my homework at the kitchen table with everybody else! I had a desk! My very own desk! My mother, surprisingly, did not demand that I return the gift, recognizing that it was a practical tool for a college student. I would find out soon after that it all came at a very large price.

Wayne insisted on being with me all the time. He didn't like my friends and refused to socialize with them. We only went out with his friends, most of whom were married with children.

Wayne was three years older than I, and his friends even older. I found myself socializing in bars and in the homes of his acquaintances—single, divorced, and married but definitely not an appropriate crowd for me.

He was also insistent about wanting to get to know my family quickly. I didn't want him to. We had been dating for four months and Thanksgiving was approaching. He started to hint at invitations to dinner with my family on Bald Eagle Road that holiday.

My family was not the sort that left the front door open and an extra plate set for an unexpected guest. If my parents had people over for dinner or an evening social event, it did not involve any extra young, single adults. We certainly were never encouraged to invite our friends into the midst of a family meal. Thus, I ignored his hints.

At noon, I was in the kitchen peeling the five pounds of potatoes that would accompany the turkey along with many other side dishes for our festive meal. As my sisters and I completed cooking, and mashing, and basting, and slicing, and the rest of our preparations, the meal was just about ready to be put on the table. Suddenly the doorbell rang.

My mother, in the living room, was the first to the front door. I heard her say with an edge to her voice, "Judy, your "friend' is here, and he brought a trumpet." I was shocked that Wayne would show up uninvited, and with a band instrument, no less. Maybe he thought he was going to play for his supper.

In fact, this young man who spent all of his earnings on his nice apartment and cars apparently had no money to spare for a decent pair of pants or a freshly laundered shirt. He was in rags . . . but he had his trumpet. I was humiliated for him and for myself. My parents were both angry that we had an interloper for dinner. We shuffled the chairs at the already crowded table to make room, and Wayne sat himself at the head of the table, my father's chair! We all gasped, and I said, "Wayne, why don't you come over and sit near me?" He answered, "No, this is good right here." My father angrily sat down and didn't say a word. My siblings were snickering around the table until my mother glared at each of them in turn, quickly dampening their pleasure at my cringeworthy situation.

Wayne seemed to enjoy his dinner heartily. He settled in the family room, uninvited again, with my father. Picking up my father's box of cigars, he tapped out a couple of them, lit the first, and then a second one, which he handed to my nearly apoplectic father.

My father had a strict sense of propriety and earned authority. Wayne, this unkempt and uninvited stranger, was now ensconced in

my father's den, awkwardly smoking and choking on Phillies Pana-
tellas. Once again, there were family conventions and norms, and
these were clearly being violated by a socially awkward individual.

I writhed in discomfort as I cleared the table along with my
snickering sisters. I headed to the kitchen to load the dishwasher
and glanced backward, hoping that Wayne would take a hint from
my florid-faced father and join me in the kitchen. I hurried as fast
as I could to finish my chores, and then left the house with Wayne
in his shiny new Satellite Sebring (with payments in default). I have
seldom been so embarrassed in my life as I was by Wayne's pre-
sumption of a Thanksgiving dinner invitation that had not been
issued by my family.

We left Weymouth and drove to Braintree to Wayne's well-ap-
pointed apartment. I sank into the plush couch, placed my purse on
an Ethan Allen side table, which held an expensive Stiffel lamp, and
finally relaxed. He poured me a glass of wine, and I felt the freedom
that I never felt at home. It was intoxicating—the freedom, that is.
There were no parents to yell at me, no chores to do, no siblings'
diapers to change, and all the privacy that we could want.

It never occurred to me, even as a straight-A student, that
something wasn't adding up with this picture. Wayne was a shoe
salesman, and one who was about to be fired from Grants at that.
I hadn't given any consideration to how he could possibly be paying rent, keeping expensive cars, and buying me lavish gifts on a
limited hourly wage. I guess I didn't really want to think about it.

What I did not know at the time but became privy to through
bits of information that would have been very disturbing when I
first knew him was that his alcoholism, escalating at his young age
of 20, was possibly secondary to childhood trauma; he had a dis-
honorable discharge from the Navy; and he had been diagnosed at
some point with schizoaffective disorder.

I loved his very sweet mother. She had all of this information
and tried at times to inform me about his background, but she felt
that she was being disloyal to her son. She never told me any of this
until much of it had been brought to my attention by him when he
was drunk.

His true financial status, belied by the expensive cars and en-
viable housing, also came to light as our time together increased.
When I was at the apartment, I would see all the demand notes for

payment of numerous revolving credit bills. There were phone calls day and night from bill collectors. Wayne assured me that he had the money, and that he was simply forgetful about paying on time. I allowed myself to believe the lies, as he was a likeable guy, and I really loved his residence and his automobiles. Shallow, yes, but I had the space and attention that I had never had as one of the oldest in a family of seven kids. And yes, I lived to regret it, but not until after I married Wayne.

His unpredictable behaviors became more apparent as the months went by. His drinking was a problem, and he began to demand more and more of my attention. I was at my family's home in my bedroom doing homework one night when he called me. I had my own phone because, unlike him, I bought very little with my earnings from my part-time jobs, and I paid cash for whatever I bought. My phone rang as I was studying for an exam. I answered to hear Wayne's slurred speech muttering that he was in my neighborhood and wanted me to come out with him. I refused, citing my school obligations, and he hung up the phone.

The phone rang every 10 minutes or so for about 40 minutes. When I would answer it, either he would beg me to come out with him right then or he would breathe into the phone but would not talk to me. I did not give in to his demands. A couple of hours later, Wayne called, fully intoxicated. He mumbled, "I crashed my car," and then hung up.

I couldn't leave the house. It was very late, and my parents would never have permitted it. There was also a strong likelihood that he was lying just to get my attention. He could, after all, still speak, albeit drunkenly. I called his apartment a number of times and there was no answer. I finally went to bed, although I was unable to sleep.

I got up at five a.m., much earlier than I normally did for school, and left the house. Rather than going directly to Bridgewater for my classes, I drove around my neighborhood to look for any signs of a car having crashed and found it. A tree on the other half of the circle that made up our neighborhood had been struck. The damage to the tree was fresh and skid marks in the road approaching the tree showed that the vehicle had attempted to avoid contact. The car that struck the tree was no longer there, but there were tire marks in the dirt indicating that the car had backed away from the tree. I had not heard any emergency vehicles during the night, but I was scared.

I drove as quickly as possible to Braintree instead of to Bridge-water. I got to his apartment, and on the side street next to the house was his badly damaged car. The damage was to the passenger side and rear of the car, with no damage to the driver's side.

Furious with what he had apparently done to get my attention, I knocked on the door. It took a while, but he answered it, looking not much the worse for wear. He was still drunk. I didn't speak to him, but immediately got back into my own car and went to school.

Nothing came of the damage to the tree. I imagine that residents of the adjoining street must have called the police when they heard the apparent collision. There was never anything in the local news about an accident during the night on Great Republic Avenue. Wayne was visibly uninjured, and I was enraged.

I ignored his calls for a few days, but we still worked in the same store. I couldn't avoid seeing him when we were scheduled for the same evening or Saturday hours. I didn't want to talk to him, but he approached me at work about a week after the collision and invited me for a ride in his brand-new royal blue Satellite Sebring Plus automobile. I had seen it in the Grants parking lot in his usual space. I asked him about the damaged vehicle, and he said that the dealership that sold him the new car had taken the badly scratched and dented car in trade—for a value that reflected the significant damage to the car.

I blame my age and lack of life experience for forgiving him and continuing our relationship despite the accident that was clearly his fault. Somewhat chagrined and yet eager to show off his car, he humbly asked me to forgive him. We continued our relationship.

This was 1972, the fall semester of my freshman year. Immediately prior to Christmas, Wayne presented me with a half-carat diamond engagement ring. I turned it down. I had not immediately succumbed to his wishes, so he broke up with me posthaste.

I should have thanked my lucky stars and run away as far as I could get, but I didn't. I was too immature to really understand the possible consequences of being in a relationship that was beyond my capacity to understand or, more, to fix.

Instead, I convinced myself that I was truly in love. Stupid.

The likelihood was that I was not thinking clearly, given that I had just had the relationship abruptly ended and felt that I "had" to get him back. It is likely that what I was really mourning was the loss of the fancy cars, the nice apartment, and the independence from my family.

The choice was "between the devil and the deep blue sea." In other words, I was facing a choice that was, to me, between two equally unpleasant courses of action. I could stay unattached and continue to live at home, in what I was finding to be too restrictive an atmosphere. I was 18. I thought I knew everything. I chose what I thought was freedom. I agreed to marry Wayne, and I packed my bags and moved out of the family home. We were married by a justice of the peace in March of 1973. My mother pointed out to me that my wedding day was actually *on* the Ides of March! She knew that a Latin scholar like me (who had studied the language for six years) would understand the implicit, well-known admonition to "Beware the Ides of March."

But there I was, married at 18, in college, working part-time and with a deadbeat husband. And of course, the story continues: he was most often out of work, fired time after time, primarily for showing up at work intoxicated. He got into drunk-driving crashes, fortunately injuring no one else.

In one of his accidents in yet another brand-new and very expensive Chrysler Cordoba LeBaron, with side opera lights and a white vinyl roof, he drove drunk on the side of the highway. He peeled off the right side of the roof when he lost control and ended up underneath the back of a disabled 18-wheeler truck.

Wayne was arrested at the scene and taken into custody. I was absolutely humiliated to have to call my father to bail him out and pay his court fees. I was shocked that my father encouraged me to "go easy on Wayne." And I still didn't divorce him.

When Wayne went to court, I had little concern for the outcome. I decided to go to the tow yard in Braintree where the car had been taken after the accident. When I got to the tow yard, I found that Peter, the young man working in the yard, was a current classmate of mine. He was a kind and gentle guy with whom I was fairly good friends at school. We looked at each other with surprise. Peter asked me what I was doing there. I was too ashamed to tell this decent guy that my reckless husband had totaled our only car. I described what car I had come to see. Peter brought me to the car and asked me with great concern, "Do you know the driver?" Hanging my head in shame, I uttered, "He's my husband." Peter looked at me with pity and said, "If you had been in that car when he drove under the 18-wheeler, you would have been decapitated." I almost cried for so many reasons.

Peter then looked at me kindly and said, "Judy, you deserve better." I truly wanted to jump in his arms and say, "You're better, are you free?" But I behaved responsibly and left after paying the fees.

Now I was making choices based on my desire to go on to further schooling after college. With my multiple part-time jobs, I could afford to stay in school *if* I stayed married. I had transferred to Boston State College in 1974 and could make do without my own car, since I could commute from Braintree to Huntington Avenue in Boston by taking a bus, a train, and a trolley. Wayne and I shared the affordable rent on the apartment, and I paid for groceries. We lived minimally but I was able to get by and meet my goals. The marriage was secondary, at best, by now.

We were married for a few more years with no improvements. In the meantime, I continued going to college full-time as well as working full-time to pay off our ever-increasing bills. My saving grace was that I stayed in school, graduating with my bachelor's degree from Boston State College in 1976 and immediately going into the two-year registered nurse program at Newton-Wellesley Hospital School of Nursing.

Wayne's disastrous behavior continued, as well as his drunkenness, spurious job history, and general unreliability. He was a genial fellow who also suffered from significant mental illness.

Wayne was never abusive, but he was also never willing to get help for his psychiatric disorders and alcohol addiction. He was home less and less. When our situation was finally just more than I was willing to accept anymore, *he* asked *me* when I was going to move out! I answered, "I'm not moving out. You are." He accepted that, and soon after moved into a rooming house a few towns away.

One might wonder what took me so long to end the marriage. There are many reasons that I can identify for staying with him so long. One was that I was never going to go back to the family home with my tail between my legs and be subjected to family rules at age 23. The second was that I was building my education and likelihood of making it financially on my own if I could just hold out a little longer. Not long after Wayne moved out, I finished nursing school, took the Massachusetts Registered Nurse Board certification exam, and got a full-time job to go along with my part-time job. I chose my own apartment, furnished it the way I wanted the most—and I had freedom.

16

⤳

Harvard Community Health Plan

H arvard Community Health Plan was one of the earliest examples of socialized medicine in the United States. HCHP was founded in 1969 by Dr. Joseph Dorsey and Maurice Lazarus and was based on the Health Insurance Plan of Greater New York and on California's Kaiser Permanente. I was introduced to this form of medical care when I became a patient in the Kenmore office of Harvard Community Health Plan.

The model for HCHP was the "health maintenance organization" (HMO), in which preventive measures were taken to maintain health. This contrasted with the former modality in medicine, which was referred to generally as the engineering model of medicine, or the "find it and fix it model." The engineering model left the patient uninvolved with health care until some disease or disorder was discovered when a patient came into a doctor's office with concerning symptoms. For instance, a patient who had not been feeling well for some period of time might go for a yearly physical and be found to have hypertension, i.e., high blood pressure. The engineering model would call for the physician to prescribe antihypertensives, and to recommend that the patient reduce their consumption of salt. The preventive model instead called for scheduled visits for routine blood pressure monitoring. If the patient was found early on to have slightly elevated blood pressure, they might or might not be prescribed antihypertensive medication, but the health care provider would advise the patient to cut down on salt intake, increase exercise, and would advocate for weight to be reduced and maintained at a level that did not contribute to hypertension or other diseases affected by caloric intake.

Health promotion and disease prevention are the foundations on which HMOs were based. Thus, a determination of overall health status incorporates the contribution of factors such as Body Mass Index (BMI) on to disease development. Patients have their BMI calculated, and health education is, ideally, provided to the patient by a team of practitioners ranging from physician to nurse to nutritionist to exercise physiologist. It's a team model, with equal weight given to the contributions of everyone on the team, including the "client" (as distinguished from the term "patient," considered a more passive term for the individual, who has a central role in the health-care team.)

HMO medical care is ostensibly provided at lower cost so that all members of a HMO group or plan are covered for all medical care. Harvard Community Health Plan, of which I was a member, and later an employee as well, had urban centers in Kenmore Square, Roxbury, and Cambridge.

For example, in the HCHP of 1974, there were no charges to the patient beyond the copay, even if that visit called for diagnostic testing and treatment outside of the primary-care physician visit. In addition to primary care physicians, all of whom were faculty members at Harvard University School of Medicine, nurse practitioners performed primary care as well.

I was beyond impressed by this slowly advancing philosophy of health and wellness care. I wanted a job at HCHP badly, but job openings were scant at the level for which I was qualified, medical expediter.

On my first visit to HCHP, I came into the building to face a long counter with employees sitting in one of six side-by-side spots. The lines each had only two or three patients waiting to be called up to the desk. This was distinctly different from any other health-care facility in which I had ever sought medical care. Even with an appointment, one would be directed to sit and wait to be called to check in. Waits were typically 15 to 30 minutes. Once checked in by secretarial staff, one was directed to sit again and wait to be called by medical staff. The model of hurry up and wait continued: after being taken into an examining room, a medical assistant would take a patient's history and current complaints, check weight and vital signs, and direct the patient to change into a flimsy garment referred to as a "johnny." The patient would then sit up on the examining table until the physician came in for the formal medical visit. Which could take quite awhile!

Differences at Harvard Community Health Plan were that patients would be checked in at the front desk and given a receipt (my copay was two dollars in 1976 for an office visit). There were no extra charges if the doctor referred you for any other services, such as radiology or specialty care, all within the same building. If you were sent on to triage (typically used for patients without a scheduled appointment, most often an urgent care visit) the cost was the same. Information was taken by a medical assistant, nurse practitioner, or directly by the physician. Another difference between HCHP and other outpatient clinics was that HCHP only accepted their own members. They did not provide care for walk-ins.

Immediately, I decided that I wanted to work there as soon as possible, and not at some vague time in the future when I might or might not decide to become a nurse practitioner. I wanted to work there right away in whatever capacity they would have me.

I compiled my resume, which included having worked for four years as a nurses' aide in three local nursing homes. I would not use the same skill set that I had acquired doing bedside patient care, but I had learned much about providing daily preventive as well as palliative care to an elderly population. Additionally, I had studied medical terminology. My six years' study of Latin certainly complemented my understanding of medical argot (i.e., the jargon used by a particular type or group of people).

I contacted the Office of Human Resources at HCHP to discuss possible job opportunities for me. I was counseled that I would certainly be qualified to be a medical expediter, but that job openings were much desired and rarely available. I volunteered that I would be willing to work in any of the three centers. Ruth, the hiring manager, laughed politely at my eagerness for employment at HCHP and advised me to call often to check to see if any opportunities for me had arisen.

Poor Ruth. I called every single Monday for a year. One

Monday, I didn't have to call Ruth. She called me. Pleasantly she told me, "Judy, I have a job for you at Kenmore." I was ecstatic. I desperately knew that I wanted to work there.

In the time that I worked as a medical expediter (gathering patient information and possibly also doing the tasks of a medical assistant in the examination room), the primary job was to extract the most relevant information to expedite care able to be provided most often by either nurse practitioners (a relatively new model of advanced nursing practice in the early 1970s) or physicians.

If a medical expediter was assigned to the triage unit, we saw unscheduled members requiring care, but another significant part of the job was taking phone calls, gathering essential information, prioritizing patients by the gravity of their medical position, and bringing them in for care. This was a relatively smooth process. Only once was I flummoxed by a medical situation, and even the nurse practitioners and physicians on duty did not have an immediate answer for me to this patient's request.

The Kenmore Square facility of HCHP occupied the first four floors of a large apartment building. While it might have been extremely convenient for residents to receive their medical care in the same building in which they lived, that was only allowed if the patient was a member of Harvard Community Health Plan, and they were only ever seen once they were checked in and matched with their computerized medical record.

One Saturday afternoon I was working, and I received a frantic call. It was from a man who lived in the apartment complex above the clinic who asked if he could be seen by a doctor immediately. I asked if he were an HCHP member. He said, "No, but this is an emergency." I recommended that he immediately go to one of the many highly esteemed Boston hospitals in the immediate area. He said insistently, "No. I need to be seen this minute." I asked him the nature of his complaint and he wouldn't tell me, but he was apparently in pain, by the sound of his voice. I asked him to hold, dashed into the provider's area, and explained the situation. One of the male nurse practitioners said wisely, "Let me take the phone call." He took the phone, spoke with the man, and said to me, "He will be here in a couple of minutes. I will provide his care and then I will have to work out with the finance department how he is to pay." The NPs, the other expediter, and I looked at him with curiosity. He quietly explained, "I am not sure how it happened, but the patient coming in just ironed his penis and is suffering from burns." The nurse practitioner blushed from embarrassment himself and quickly went into an examining room to await the patient. He poked his head out the door for a moment and coughed uncomfortably as he asked me if I would quickly go to the employee lunchroom and bring back a large bag of ice. I did so.

I didn't have to question the hobbling man who came into the triage area. It was pretty obvious what part of him was injured. I led him into the exam room where the nurse practitioner awaited him. We were all curious but too professional to ask questions of any kind. Soon thereafter, the patient left the room, hurrying back to the elevator to return to his apartment (and hopefully not to finish his ironing). Nothing more was ever spoken about the event, except, I imagine, by the finance department, trying to figure out how to bill the patient, who hopefully would not iron while nude again.

I worked at Harvard Community Health Plan during my senior year in college and until after I graduated from Newton-Wellesley Hospital and passed my board of registration in nursing. I was now a nurse with no home. I had worked hard for my diploma, and I needed to be employed full-time as a registered nurse immediately.

I was hired at Quincy City Hospital, at that time an old hospital staffed with old doctors practicing using antiquated ideas, beliefs, and attitudes toward nurses. I was suddenly thrown back in time and found myself reclassified as "handmaiden to physician."

I tried blending the old with the new, working in a very traditional hospital, likely with its original equipment and philosophies of care. I also kept my evening job as a medical expediter at HCHP, where I was very happy but overqualified and underpaid for my particular position. Reluctantly, I soon had to give up my much-loved HCHP job and take a job as a traditional registered nurse, for which I had specifically trained. I decided that I had to focus on nursing and my further education rather than staying static at HCHP. If I did decide to become a nurse practitioner, I would once again seek employment at Harvard Community Health Plan. Time would tell.

17

✍

Newton-Wellesley Hospital School of Nursing

The Newton-Wellesley Hospital School of Nursing in Newton was one of the highest-ranked registered nurse programs in Massachusetts, and although not an easy commute, the stellar reputation of the school made it an easy choice for me to attend.

I knew that Newton-Wellesley favored college graduates for admission to their two-year RN diploma program. Credits from Boston State College would not be transferable, but I was well prepared with my bachelor's degree that demonstrated that half of my credits were in the life sciences. I applied and was accepted.

I was a bit nervous: this was the first time I would have to take a loan to pay my tuition. But I would continue working part-time to pay for living expenses and was confident I would be able to pay off my tuition loan with the job opportunities and steady income available to new registered nurses at the time.

Although I was in an ever-weakening marriage, I did not have children, nor did I plan any. I made the conscious decision to stay living in our apartment in Braintree from which I had been able to commute by bus, train, and trolley to Boston State. The same public transportation system that afforded me access to Boston State College from Braintree brought me—with an additional half-hour on the Riverside trolley rather than the Huntington Avenue trolley, plus a very short walk—to the hospital school and hospital where I would do my clinical rotations.

With such a long commute, it became old hat to read my school assignments while bouncing in bus, train, and trolley seats, as I had during the three legs of my public transportation journey to Boston State College.

Fortunately, a short time into my career at Newton-Wellesley, I met Patty, a fellow student who also lived in Braintree. She was amenable to driving me to school in exchange for gas money. As I was still working part-time at Harvard Community Health Plan in Kenmore Square, on the nights that I worked after school, I simply changed trolleys at Park Street and rode the line to the Fenway Park-area health-care facility. Following work at HCHP late in the evening, I returned to Kenmore Square and took the trolley to Park Street, transferred to the Red Line to Quincy Square, and then took the Quincy Avenue bus that dropped me off just across the street from the Braintree apartment.

Many of my classmates at NWHSON were also college graduates. I had found in my research on nursing schools that different institutions focused on different populations of potential students. Newton-Wellesley was one of the few diploma programs that accepted significantly more college graduates.

While I was in traditional college environments, my friends attending diploma and associate degree programs in nursing, on hearing of my ambitions, warned me incessantly that traditional nursing schools were *nothing like* regular college. I disputed this— and was proven wrong. Traditional nursing schools did *not* believe in democracy and negotiation. For nursing instructors in schools such as Newton-Wellesley, it was "my way or the highway." Fairness had no place in nursing training.

We older, educated, and emboldened college graduates were not as malleable as the younger NWHSON students directly out of high school, or the numerous mothers who had not attended nursing school until after their children were raised. We often made quite vocal objections to what we perceived as the unfair demands of the nursing instructors. My demographic was loud and proud— and more likely to be shown the door if our protestations against policies and practices mandated by our training program were even questioned.

Patty, my commuting partner, had trained and been in practice as a licensed practical nurse at Newton-Wellesley Hospital prior to enrolling in the registered nurse program at the hospital school. For two years, she warned me, "Judy, watch your mouth and your attitude. You are going to get thrown out."

I never did get thrown out. Instead, both my dear friend Lori and I, who was as mouthy as I was, almost got dismissed from the school within two short months of graduation.

Lori and I were at the head of the class academically in the nursing program, along with our even louder and more abrasive friend Ronnie. However, the three of us often went just short of "too far" in our encounters with the militaristic nursing instructors.

I had met Lori during the first few weeks of nursing school. I was sitting behind her in the lecture hall, which barely contained the school's approximately 90 students in attendance. I noticed as I sat behind Lori with Patty (who was always quiet and respectful) that Lori kept tugging at her blouse, pulling it down and tucking it under her skirt. I recognized the motion and leaned forward, whispering to this woman I had yet to meet, "Don't worry, your shirt is covering your ass."

Rather than abruptly angering and turning to face backward in her seat, Lori erupted into loud laughter, causing me to do the same. Although we were seated at the very back of the classroom, our guffaws were audible to the nursing instructor in the front of the room. She stopped the lecture and glared in our direction. As newcomers to the school, that was enough to silence the two of us. After class we grabbed each other by the arms and she asked me, "How did you know that I was self-conscious about my shirt being tucked under my butt at all times when I am sitting?" I answered her, "Because my butt is bigger than yours, and I always do the same thing." (As if we could hide our ample rear ends with a shirttail!)

Although near-strangers an hour previously, we instantly knew that we were meant to be close friends. Most of the other students in our nursing school cohort ignored our hysteria. But Ronnie approached us in the student lounge immediately after class and said in a heavy Bronx accent, "Hey, you guys. I want to be a part of this!" Thus, we became the trio Ronnie christened Large (Lori), Extra Large (me), and Jumbo (herself). For the remaining members of the class, we were known as the often obnoxious but comical students who put the entire class in jeopardy of additional punitive assignments.

As silly as the three of us were for the entire two years of nursing school, we retained our status because we excelled grade-wise and performed our clinical tasks with professionalism and courtesy to our patients.

However, as we advanced in the program, we became even bolder. Lori and I walked a fine line. But Ronnie perceived no such line and would frequently respond to nursing instructors' directives to do things such as work extra evening clinical rotations without notice with vocal objections. She would call across the crowded classrooms, "*We are consumers. We have our rights!*"

Ronnie was not the only student who acted inappropriately at times. There were about a dozen in our student body who gave the nursing instructors chills when they raised their hands to speak in class. Sometimes what came out of a student's mouth was quickly quashed by nursing instructors who had learned to thrust and parry with the most entitled students.

For example, one student's comment left everyone in the room speechless, teacher as well as fellow students. Often, we would have guests come to speak to our assembled class. When we were studying insulin-dependent diabetes mellitus (IDDM), one of the school's administrators invited a neighbor of hers with the infirmity to speak to us. The neighbor was more than willing to talk to us about living with the disease, also known as type 1 diabetes. The speaker was a very well-known, attractive male Boston newscaster. We were privileged that he would volunteer time out of his demanding schedule to impress upon us the ramifications of having IDDM, especially with the lifestyle he maintained.

We sat transfixed by his intelligence, charm, and willingness to answer any and all questions related to the disease he had lived with since childhood. He made the mistake after he lectured of asking us if we had any questions. Immediately, Diana, one of the bolder students in the class, raised her hand and asked him loudly, "Do you often have problems with impotence?" As a class, we gasped in horror. To his credit, he maintained his calm and simply answered, "Fortunately, no." He didn't have to say anything more to her. As soon as class ended, our nursing instructor and half the students in class converged on her and let her know without question how rudely she had treated the speaker.

But Ronnie went far further than Lori or I could even imagine when we had a full-day lecture at a local cancer hospital. We were not involved with patients at the hospital. Instead, we were assembled there for a full morning lecture by the revered hospital chief of medicine, Dr. Hirohito.

One thing that our older and more educated body of students felt strongly, compared with traditional younger nursing students who were right out of high school and much more subdued, was that we were all entitled consumers. We recognized at the same time that we had given up a lot of our autonomy when we entered the hallowed halls of a traditional nursing school.

Our older student body vociferously objected to the image of nurses as subservient to physicians or anybody else! We were professionals. Approximately 85 percent of our class were females. However, male nursing students were treated with more deference by both older nursing instructors and by patients, who assumed the male students to be physicians.

On the day of our lecture, we assembled at the cancer hospital and proceeded to the hall where Dr. Hirohito would lecture and then take questions. The didactic method required that we as a body participate in the exercise. Primarily that meant that Dr. Hirohito would show us slides of body parts exhibiting various manifestations of cancer. He would respectfully direct the students to consider what the slides might be depicting. If no one would answer out of fear of being wrong, he would encourage us to make an educated guess at what we were seeing on the slides.

The class soon was taken aback by the simpering behavior of the registered nurse who was the doctor's assistant. She all but curtsied when he came to the front of the lecture hall, asked him if he was comfortable, and attempted even to fluff the absent cushions in his nearby chair.

Ronnie announced *sotto voce* that she was incensed by the extreme devotion of this registered nurse to her "higher being." Unfortunately, Ronnie was naturally loud, even when attempting to whisper. Ronnie, Lori, and I were seated together, and within a short period of time, Ronnie made yet another rude comment audible to increasing numbers of our classmates.

Lori and I took turns poking and then pinching Ronnie as her behavior became intolerable in a professional setting. Ronnie retorted loudly to our warnings that she "had her rights," and if she objected to the demeaning behavior of Dr. Hirohito's nurse-assistant, then that was her prerogative!

There was no containing the irascible Ronnie. At one point, Dr. Hirohito was projecting slides depicting various growths and physical abnormalities on parts of bodies. Out of respect for the patients whose tumors had been photographed, the faces were never shown in the slides. However, there was a picture of a neck with a malignancy present. In the slide, a tool was used to demonstrate the relative size of the growth. Dr. Hirohito directed us to identify the malady. No one would volunteer an answer as this was something that none of us had encountered in any of our patients. Dr. Hirohito's assistant became anxious when no one volunteered a response and she pleaded, "Somebody answer the question!" She went up to the screen on which the image was portrayed, pointed to the growth, and said, "Anybody? An educated guess?" Ronnie, annoyed as hell by now due to the cloying behavior of the woman, refused to contain herself any longer.

Silence continued to greet the assistant. In frustration, she demanded, "Somebody, tell Dr. Hirohito what you see on the slide!" Ronnie called out, "It looks like a ruler to me," referring to the measuring tool in the photo. We all gasped, while Ronnie could barely keep herself in her seat. Her raucous laughter shook her whole body. The woman on the stage was holding back tears of frustration at this point.

Lori and I grimaced and leaned over Ronnie, telling her, "That's enough! Everybody is fully aware that you have no respect for Dr. Hirohito or his assistant. Just shut up!" Ronnie shrugged but complied with us.

Within ten minutes, as the lecture continued, Ronnie noisily reached into her backpack and pulled out a paper bag. From each side, Lori and I simultaneously kicked her and whispered quietly, "Whatever it is that you intend to do, cut it out!" She whined, "But I'm hungry!" The paper bag rustled as she removed a smelly cheese and onion sandwich and bit into it.

Dr. Hirohito's assistant was enraged. She bustled quickly to where the three of us were sitting, leaned over Lori, and demanded of Ronnie, "*What are you doing?*"

Ronnie replied matter-of-factly, "I am a diabetic; I have to eat right now." Feeling embarrassed from seeming to have called unnecessary attention to Ronnie's illness, the woman apologized profusely. Ronnie responded, "No problem," and continued to chomp her sandwich with an open mouth.

Knowing that Ronnie was, in fact, not diabetic, Lori and I pinched her hard, and she laughed out loud. Other students started to whisper furiously to Lori and me to "get her to shut up and stop acting like an idiot." We were actually helpless to anticipate her misbehavior or to stop it. We thought that Ronnie would behave like a respectful adult now that she had rudely interrupted the diagnostic assessment part of the cancer lecture.

Within a short period, the class recessed for lunch. Lori and I wanted to run out of the room, but Ronnie was taking her time packing her bag. Within moments, the nearly defeated assistant approached Ronnie apologetically. Lori and I grimaced as she walked toward us, knowing that this portended something even worse than what Ronnie had already done. The woman gently said to Ronnie, "I wonder if I could talk to you for a few moments. My sister was just diagnosed with diabetes, and I'd like to ask you for advice."

"*No, no, no!*" Lori and I inwardly screamed. "Please don't let this be happening!" Ronnie answered matter-of-factly, "I was only kidding. I don't have diabetes. I was just hungry."

The poor woman nearly fell to the floor in despair over Ronnie's inexcusable reply. At that point, Lori and I were tempted to slap Ronnie. Instead, I said, "I am so sorry. Ronnie has Tourette's Syndrome."

While I had compounded the lie with another lie, the woman gratefully accepted my explanation. Lori and I resisted the urge to clap our hands over Ronnie's mouth, but we did forcefully drag her from the room, into her vehicle, and sent her home.

Our nursing instructors who had accompanied us to Dr. Hirohito's lecture called to us from the parking lot, where some of them had given in to a usually repressed urge to smoke a cigarette, "Get Ronnie out of here." Lori and I were excused from the afternoon segment of the lecture, likely because of our association with Ronnie.

From what we heard the next day, Dr. Hirohito's afternoon lecture was extremely informative and much appreciated by the rest of Newton-Wellesley Hospital's nursing class. Apparently, Ronnie's absence was celebrated for the rest of the day.

The incidents were never mentioned again. Ronnie actually deserved expulsion for her atrocious behavior that day but recalling her frequent strident objection—"We are consumers! We have rights!"—our faculty apparently took the high (and easier) road, and the incidents of that morning were never spoken of again. Until now.

Because of the intensity of learning how to provide health care to often critically ill patients, as students we were terrified of making errors. We were cautioned again and again that if we were not sure of information, we should look it up or ask an instructor. We had many lectures on proper comportment as registered nurses in training. Much of the time we were focused on the psychological needs of the patient and family, as well as the disease processes and surgical procedures.

Roger, one of the older male students from our class, was caring but loud. He was cautioned again and again to use appropriate medical terminology with the patients, and then always to ask if those for whom he was providing care had any questions. When he was assigned to his clinical rotation in the emergency room, he was in his second year of our two-year program and presumed to be proficient in the tasks he was given. One morning, his patient was a young man who had been in a serious car accident. Roger worked with the team to assess the patient, take him for diagnostic tests, medicate the patient as ordered, and keep the young man as comfortable as possible. The young man had come into the hospital by ambulance, arriving about an hour before his family got to the ER. As the patient had been diagnosed with a neck fracture, he had been transported to the orthopedic unit on the fourth floor for application of skeletal traction to stabilize his neck. The traction required that medical bolts be inserted into his skull and attached to a metal ring that encircled his head so that he couldn't further exacerbate the injury.

While the patient was still in the orthopedic unit, his parents and siblings came running into the ER crying loudly, asking where the patient could be found. They had no idea at that time what his injuries were. Roger was helping to care for other ER patients until the neck injury patient was transported back downstairs. Roger heard the commotion and called across the unit to the nearly hysterical family, "Don't worry! Your son is upstairs getting fitted for his halo." The family screamed, the mother fainted, and Roger's nursing instructor ran to the family, calling loudly, "He is in the fourth-floor orthopedic unit being fitted for a device called 'halo traction,' which stabilizes the head and neck to prevent further injury!"

It took quite a bit of comforting to reassure the family that the patient was alive, conscious, and medically stable (and not in Heaven). Roger was summarily removed from his rotation in the emergency room, only to have to do one-on-one training with the supervisor of nursing in order to complete his nursing school education.

Leaving us both with mixed emotions many years later was an event from our nursing school education involving Lori and me. I had been assigned to a patient who was coming into Newton-Wellesley Hospital for an outpatient procedure. She was to have a colonoscopy with very light sedation. I was asked to stay in the procedure room with her, essentially to hold her hand and make her feel more comfortable. I came into the small room and introduced myself to Julianne, a woman in her mid-50s. We instantly bonded. I interviewed her as part of my training, but she (like me) was a chatterer. We also both responded to nervousness with laughter. I explained the procedure that the gastroenterologist was about to perform, and we got a bit giggly. When she reached out and grabbed my hand and asked, "Will you stay with me?" I assured her that I would be standing at her head while the procedure was being performed and would stay until she was ready to go home.

During the procedure, I saw the gastroenterologist's grim look as he encountered a large colorectal tumor and did a biopsy. I continued to distract Julianne, as it was apparent she wanted to feel like she was anywhere but in this room. We chatted some more, still laughing and telling amusing stories to each other, and then the physician left the room. He told her he would call her at home with her results. Julianne got dressed and I took her down to the waiting area, where her husband was anxious to take her home.

As a student, it was part of my assignment to follow up on the results of the test and to write a paper for my clinical instructor. I was horrified when I saw the results. Julianne had an inoperable colorectal tumor with a very poor prognosis. She was admitted to the hospital a week later and requested that I be assigned to her on the inpatient unit. I happily accepted the assignment and went in and hugged her immediately.

Julianne kept up her own spirits by sharing jokes with me, talking about family, and generally focusing on anything but her plight. At times, I would ask her, "Is there anything you want to talk about?" I knew from the shift reports that Julianne had been told she had a short time to live, but she chose to spend any time that we were together laughing and telling stories. I discussed this with my nursing instructor, who advised me that since Julianne saw her doctor and her primary care nurses every day, she was fully informed that she had very little time left. She wanted her time with me to be just lighthearted. One day, early in her hospitalization, I brought Lori in to meet her after clinical ended. Julianne loved Lori too, as we all had similar senses of humor. We chatted and laughed but left opportunities for serious talk should Julianne want to engage us.

I encountered a conundrum one day as Julianne held my hand. I was wearing a sapphire ring whose center stone was surrounded by diamond chips. It was a family ring that had been given to me and I treasured it. Julianne noticed the ring and said, "Judy, I love this. I want it!" I struggled with my emotions. I felt that I should give it to her, but it was a precious gift to me. I looked at Lori for an indication of what I should do. She looked at me wide-eyed and shrugged her shoulders. I would happily have allowed Julianne to wear my ring for some specified period of time, but she didn't have a specified period of time to live. If I put it on her finger, it would be lost to me. I agonized over the decision, and finally had to say to her, "Why don't you wear it every time that I am in the room with you, and then I will take it home with me when I leave?" She giggled and said, "No. I want to keep it." But I quietly stuck by my (in)decision and let her wear it while I was with her.

School vacation week came, and Lori and I went in together to see Julianne. We didn't mention it to our instructors, fearing that we would be chastised for not maintaining a professional distance from a patient. Julianne was as happy to see us as we were to see her. We hugged. We all held back our tears, even though it was clear that Julianne did not have much time left. School vacation ended, and I was once again assigned to Julianne. Lori came in during our shift to visit Julianne, and we said, "Aren't you going to wear the ring today?" She looked wanly at us and said, "I'd love to."

Julianne was there the next day, but not the day after. She had passed during the night. I still have the ring, but after Julianne died, I put it in my jewelry box and didn't wear it again. When I look at it after all these years, I see Julianne's smiling face and remember the camaraderie that helped us all to experience her dying and her death within the circle of that ring and our shared laughter.

18

❧

The Blizzard of '78

The Blizzard of 1978 was a catastrophic nor'easter that formed on Sunday, February 5, 1978, and ended two days later. Snow fell from Monday morning, February 6, straight through to the evening of Tuesday, February 7. Massachusetts, Rhode Island, and Connecticut were especially hard hit by this storm, which left Boston with a record-breaking 27.1 inches of snow. (Providence was hit even harder than Boston with 27.6 inches of snow.) Nearly all economic activity was disrupted in the worst-hit areas. The storm killed about 100 people in the Northeast overall and injured about 4,500. It caused more than $520 million in damage.

Numerous power outages ensued from the strong winds and extremely heavy precipitation. The zero visibility severely impacted travelers, many of whom were commuting to work, school, and elsewhere when the most snow was falling. By the time it ended, thousands of people were stranded and homeless.

The Blizzard of '78 brought heavy snow for 33 hours, compared to the average time of 6 to 12 hours of snow falling.

One of the major problems with the Blizzard of 1978 was that because snow failed to arrive in Monday's predawn hours as predicted, many people believed that the storm had gone out to sea.

Despite ominous predictions by National Weather Service forecasters, people went to work and school as usual. The delayed storm, with its unusual ferocity, left people unprepared for its devastating effects.

While many workers were allowed by employers to stay at home, many categories of workers, including nurses, were considered "essential employees," and expected to make it to work, and to stay, even in worsening storm conditions. Nursing students were in this category as well.

At Newton-Wellesley Hospital School of Nursing, my classmates and I went to school as expected on Monday morning, February 6. Patty and I commuted in her Volkswagen Beetle, leaving for school by 6:30 a.m. We drove from Braintree to Newton Lower Falls, where the school was located, a distance of 22 miles, by way of backroads and then mostly highway. The typical commuting time from Braintree to school was 35 minutes or so.

As we began our journey, we weren't too concerned about the storm. We, along with nearly all of our classmates, arrived in class on time. The storm was the early morning topic of conversation, but we had arrived, and we all planned to stay until our usual dismissal time of 3:30 p.m.

While our nursing school instructors were lecturing, more and more students were soon looking out the window at the dismal conditions than toward the front of the classroom. A few students raised their hands and asked for permission to leave early because the storm was very visibly worsening. As expected, our instructor answered with a laugh, "Nurses never leave their posts."

While I, along with Lori and Ronnie, had a reputation for challenging our faculty with cause, the instructors did not usually believe that we would try anything that seemed like even mild insurrection. And Patty did not fit the "challenging" category by any stretch of the imagination. Patty was already a licensed practical nurse and had been working at Newton-Wellesley when she decided to advance in her chosen career. She entered the registered nurse program with my class, although with a much more worldly understanding of what employment in the health-care field truly demanded.

My class continued to grumble about being held in classes as the storm picked up rapidly. The instructors became more adamant that *no one* was going anywhere until the established class dismissal time.

Patty, however, was more than six months pregnant. She stood up in the middle of class, looked at the instructor, and said, "I am very sorry to disobey you, but Judy and I are leaving. We have the longest commute, and I am not going to endanger my baby's health." Patty, of course, said this with the utmost respect. I gladly grabbed my coat and left with her. The instructor was furious and said grudgingly to the rest of the class, "I am not going to prevent a pregnant woman from leaving, but the rest of you are staying!"

This was a disastrous decision on the part of the nursing instructor. Patty and I had a treacherous ride home from the moment we got into her car until we arrived home. The snow seemed to be dumping out of the sky with no indication of letting up in the foreseeable future. Patty, whose house was closer to the Braintree highway exit than mine, told me that she wasn't taking any more chances driving in the blizzard. We stopped at her house, and in she went, switching places with her husband as my driver, who dropped me off at my apartment on Quincy Avenue (Route 53) in Braintree.

We were told by our classmates that a mere 20 minutes after Patty and I left school that day, official word came from the Hospital security department that the nursing school was to be closed, and all students and nonessential hospital employees were to be sent home.

As for the students who obediently stayed in class when our nursing instructor demanded they do so, some made it home that day. They were primarily the students who lived on the hospital campus in the nursing school dormitories. Like thousands of other commuters in eastern Massachusetts on February 6, 1978, a significant percentage didn't make it home until up to five days later, as they were stranded on roads made impassable by snow.

Thousands of employees throughout the storm area were sent home starting in the early afternoon of February 6. Thousands more were caught by the treacherous event. Many people were stranded in their cars along roads throughout Massachusetts and other parts of New England. Many of my classmates, relatives, and friends were marooned in their vehicles until the storm ended and roads were cleared. Those who stayed with their vehicles were in them for two to five days.

Tragically, at least 14 people died on Route I-95 near Boston because snow piled high enough to prevent poisonous exhaust fumes from escaping from their idling vehicles. Many snowbound vehicles eventually had to be evacuated by cross-country skiers and snowmobilers. Snowplows were stuck in traffic as the snow continued to fall. Jackknifed tractor trailers blocked traffic in both directions on two major Boston-area highways. The Neponset River also flooded I-93 in Milton, causing the highway's complete closure.

Throughout eastern Massachusetts, automobile traffic was banned for the remainder of the week. Thousands of people walked and skied on the quiet city streets.

Quincy Avenue in Braintree, where my apartment was located, is between Weymouth Landing and Quincy Square. Once people could get outside their homes after days of being snowbound, we found buses stranded along the length of Quincy Avenue. The snow had accumulated enough during the blizzard to have actually buried the buses. I lived on the corner of Edgehill Road, and my friends and I took pictures of each other sitting on top of the buses, street signs, and snowbanks. Those who owned snowmobiles used them freely, often to help rescue others stuck in their cars.

Snowmobiles were also employed to transport to hospitals those who had become ill or injured during the storm. Others utilized cross-country skis and sleds to get around. While there was nothing entertaining in any way about the Blizzard of 1978, my one regret is that I never kept the photographs that I took once we were no longer housebound. The image that stays firmly in my memory is that involving Norfolk Package Store at the beginning of Quincy Avenue right outside of Weymouth Landing.

Both the Town of Weymouth and the City of Quincy prohibited alcohol sales during and after the blizzard until some degree of normalcy returned. For many people, lack of access to alcohol was too much to endure after this historic storm. People walked to Braintree from Weymouth and Quincy, happy that Braintree was not "dry" as a result of the storm. Norfolk Package Store was a very small establishment, and only a few customers were typically in the store at one time. But those who wanted it were willing to wait for their favorite (or any) beer, wine, or other spirits.

The photographs that I took were of long orderly lines, primarily of men pulling children's sleds, stretching from the entry of Norfolk Package Store to the funeral home across the street. I jokingly asked a number of people in the lines how far they had walked to get to the "packy." The would-be customers actually engaged in a verbal contest to determine who had walked the farthest to do their shopping. Most had dragged the sleds without taking their children along for the ride. It was easy for me to laugh at the sight. I only had to walk about an eighth of a mile from my apartment for a bottle of wine.

Another memory that I have of the week of the Blizzard of '78 was watching the news every day and seeing our governor, Michael Dukakis, clad in comfortable sweaters while facing the camera. I had a great deal of respect for Governor Dukakis and his role in the storm, in addition to ministering to the political affairs of the state of Massachusetts. During the crisis, an essential duty of his was to be front and center on the news, reassuring the people of the Commonwealth that we were being shepherded through this crisis. To me, Governor Dukakis took on the role of our own Mister Rogers (Reverend Fred McFeely Rogers). A Presbyterian minister, Rogers earned a graduate degree in child development and created the beloved television show, *Mister Rogers' Neighborhood*. The show, which ran for 33 years, was critically acclaimed for the way it addressed children's emotional and physical concerns.

Although very differently from Mister Rogers, Governor Dukakis took to the Boston airwaves each day to provide guidance and reassurance to the people of Massachusetts that the state was doing everything in its power to restore life as usual to the people of the Commonwealth.

To me, the governor's clothing was significant on these broadcasts. Mister Rogers was known for wearing sweaters handmade by his mother on all of his televised shows. It was meant to give a homey and warm feeling to his audience.

Dukakis, broadcasting to a likely predominantly adult audience, acknowledged the severity of the storm and emphasized that the Blizzard of '78 occurred on top of a storm two weeks earlier that had left two feet of snow on the ground. When he was interviewed many years later about the Blizzard of '78, Dukakis recounted the enormous death and injury toll. And yet he had remained calm on camera, his voice unwavering, describing to a fearful audience what the Commonwealth was doing to abate the effects of the horrific storm.

19

⤳

Quincy City Hospital

I've mentioned that as soon as I received my RN, I began working at the antiquated Quincy City Hospital. It opened in 1890 as a treatment center for granite workers suffering from dust inhalation in Quincy, known as the City of Presidents. (Quincy was the birthplace of John Adams and John Quincy Adams). For its first 80 years, the hospital was owned by the city and had a prominent place on top of the hill on Whitwell Street that became known as "Hospital Hill." The hospital long served the working class. It was called by Edward Fitzgerald, president of the Quincy Historical Society, "the ordinary people's hospital."

During its greater-than-100-year history, countless births and deaths had occurred there, and many thousands of local people were diagnosed and treated. But the facility closed its doors for good in December of 2014. Over the years, the hospital had suffered many financial losses related to the steady decline in patient visits. The hospital, when I worked for it in 1978, had an overall physical structure that had become dilapidated. Surgical-5, the unit in which I worked, was still referred to as "the new building" at the time I worked there, even though it was 25 years old and poorly maintained.

Quincy City relied on old equipment and older physicians and nurses. It was a hospital to which local employees became very emotionally attached. An aspect of the facility that was both a blessing and a curse was that the hospital was so close to state-of-the-art hospitals with top-tier medical schools in Boston that people started going elsewhere for care. The hospital, despite as many updates as it could financially withstand, was left severely lacking compared to other suburban Boston hospitals such as South Shore Hospital and Brockton Hospital. Revenues began to decline precipitously, and finally the City of Quincy sold the facility to Steward Health Care. Although the acute-care community hospital had 196 patient beds and 545 workers, its finances had been unstable for years. When I was employed by the hospital from mid-1978 to late 1979, there were weeks at a time when the hospital could not meet its payroll. Frantic employees lined up at the payroll office week after week to see if there was money to fill the cash envelopes.

As well, Quincy could not keep up with many of the evolving philosophies and standards of care for its patients. At the time I was hired there, the vast majority of their registered nurses were trained in the hospital's own school of nursing. Very few of us were hired from schools other than Quincy Hospital School of Nursing, which lacked sufficient resources to upgrade medical care or teaching as the disciplines of medicine, surgery, obstetrics, and others evolved.

The hospital held on precariously in the 36 years between the time I resigned and when the hospital ultimately closed. As I had graduated from Newton-Wellesley Hospital School of Nursing after working as a medical expediter at Harvard Community Health Plan, I brought with me to Quincy City Hospital a wealth of high-quality experience and education.

A majority of the younger physicians, nurses, and allied health-care professionals had been educated at top-tier hospitals in Boston and elsewhere. The training and experiences of those from more progressive institutions often differed philosophically and qualitatively compared to Quincy Hospital's aging long-term providers.

It is imperative for the best outcomes of the patients that those providing both curative and palliative care have equivalent education, training, and philosophies of both illness and wellness.

For the nurses who worked side-by-side, the majority employed by Quincy City Hospital had received their training in the hospital's own nursing school. Unfortunately, Quincy-trained nurses often projected to those of us educated in other schools of nursing that we were "outsiders."

This resulted in a not-so-subtle differentiation between the groups, which interfered with collaborative care.

While many nurses, regardless of training institution, worked well with other caregivers, it was perceived by both groups that resentment festered. This often came about because those trained in more science-based, state-of-the-art practices felt there were qualitative differences in the care provided to patients, depending on the staff's training institutions. One particular incident I witnessed bears unfortunate testimony to this type of situation.

Most medical research agrees that the disease known as Acquired Immune Deficiency Syndrome (AIDS), which is caused by the human immunodeficiency virus (HIV), first entered the United States in 1976. Once the cause was identified, it became accepted in the United States and throughout most of the developed world. As the blood of an infected HIV patient was a major route of transmission, health-care workers were mortally afraid of contracting the disease, which had a significantly high conveyance rate, particularly with exposure to used needles and direct blood contact.

When I heard about what was then called "the gay virus" because of the number of homosexuals contracting the disease, I began to research it through the current available literature. So much was unknown about the transmissible virus with its high fatality rate that the medical communities hurried to learn as much as possible about what was called early on "human tumor leukemic virus." Within a couple of years, more and more information was discovered and disseminated about the deadly virus. The predominant methods to contain the virus that were immediately instituted included extended use of medical precautions to slow the spread of the disease and decreasing exposure to contaminated medical instruments, surfaces, and people known to have the virus. Sexual contact with an HIV-infected person introduced a very high risk of becoming HIV-positive. Additionally, those in the medical professions who were exposed to copious amounts of patients' blood (such as in obstetrical care and bone surgery), were at significant risk of contracting the virus, even when strict infection control measures were in place.

The book *And the Band Played On* was written by San Francisco-based investigative reporter Randy Shilts to examine "Politics, People, and the AIDS Epidemic," as its subtitle says. News agencies put a great deal of focus on the number of deaths throughout the world that occurred through exposure to infected blood and body fluids.

I conducted a number of continuing education lectures on HIV infection for nurses, physicians, and other health-care workers at Quincy Hospital. Most medical facilities were mounting huge campaigns to warn anyone who might be susceptible how to use medicine's "universal precautions" to avoid becoming a victim of the rarely treatable or curable virus. The media was also doing its best to spread the same message.

Not long after I presented the most up-to-date information I had researched to a group of nurses at Quincy Hospital, an RN with at least ten years' experience ran into our conference room laughing hysterically. "Guys, guys," she called to those of us enjoying our 15-minute coffee break. "You'll never believe what I did!" She held up her hands to us, holding two syringes in one of them. The other hand held only an alcohol wipe, used to prep the skin prior to injecting medication under the skin (subcutaneously, or SC) and into the muscle (intramuscularly, or IM). She continued to laugh like a hyena, and burst out saying, "You'll never believe this. I was supposed to give injections to two different patients. I gave the first guy his shot and grabbed the wrong syringe (the used one) and injected it into the second guy! I didn't want him to realize it, so I casually injected *his* syringe into the other arm, explaining [by lying to the patient] that those were the *two* shots that he was scheduled to receive." She continued to laugh and about half of our co-workers laughed along with her. No one spoke up at first. I then said, "You could have exposed him to the AIDS virus. You need to report that as a medical error so that he can be monitored for any signs of the disease." She called me a "faggot" and laughed. I reported the incident to our head nurse, who simply said, "Oh, dear. Let's hope nothing comes of this." I gave my notice of termination that afternoon. Unfortunately, this was the second time I had personally encountered an instance of egregious medical error, to which there was no corrective or even punitive response.

Two months previously, I had tried to keep my own dear uncle from even being admitted to Quincy City Hospital. My uncle Al, in his late 60s by then, had been on top of his roof in Quincy repairing shingles when he lost his footing and plunged to the ground. My aunt immediately called an ambulance, which brought him to "the

Quincy," as they had always called the hospital. I was working that day, and my aunt called my floor to tell me that my uncle was being admitted. "Aunt Loretta," I begged her, "have the ambulance take him anywhere else, but don't admit him here." She responded, "But he likes the Quincy. He's always come here." Frantic, I convinced her to request that he be admitted on the floor on which I worked, so that I could monitor his care while he was hospitalized. I visited him after my shift and told him I would check on him first thing the next morning.

The next day I came in and had to listen to shift reports before I started my work on the patient floor. As the charge nurse on nights was doing "rounds" and reporting to the incoming shift what had gone on with each patient during the preceding night, she casually said, "Oh, by the way, Mr. Struzik was accidentally overdosed on morphine during the night. They reversed him with Narcan and he's fine." I jumped up yelling, "My uncle? My uncle?" I continued, stating that I had strenuously tried to prevent him from being admitted to "the Quincy" because of the overall poor quality of care. I ran down to his room, and he was trembling in his bed. "Judy," he moaned, "I don't know what happened to me. The nurse came in to give me a shot and I told her I didn't need it. She gave it to me anyway, and suddenly I started seeing toasters and televisions and doors floating past me. I have never been so scared in my life."

The older, careless nurse simply got a syringe of Narcan, a narcotic antagonist, and left the room after patting him on the leg and telling him he'd be "fine." She never told him that she accidentally overdosed him with a narcotic medication that was never ordered by his physician, and then reversed him with another medication that was not ordered for him.

I immediately called the day supervisor and, nearly breathless, told her what the night nurse had done to my uncle. The long-term Quincy City Hospital day nursing supervisor looked at me, smiled benignly, and said, "Oh, that Madeline. What are we going to do about her?" My thought immediately was to sue her for the damage that she had caused. However, my aunt and uncle told me they "didn't want to cause any problems."

Another issue with which I had dealt repeatedly as a charge nurse at QCH concerned an impaired physician. On weekends, Dr.

Moore, an elderly physician, would come in to do rounds on his patients while clearly intoxicated. He wore his medical garb along with oversized sunglasses, as if his bloodshot eyes were the only detectable sign that he was impaired. He'd glance toward his patients' charts I had assembled for him. Without even opening them, he'd mumble to me, "Renew all of my patients' orders, would you?"

I answered, "Certainly, if you will lend me your medical license and sign over your paycheck to me." He took that to mean exactly what I had facetiously meant by it. I could see that he was glaring at me through the sunglasses, which did little to hide his red-streaked eyes. He muttered an epithet at me and stumbled his way off the unit. I had no choice but to call in another physician to review the condition of Dr. Moore's patients and renew or change their care plans.

Previously, when I had been employed as a medical expediter at the world-class Harvard Community Health Plan, highly skilled doctors, nurses, and other medical personnel loved teaching anyone who was eager to learn. I was a sponge for their willingness to mentor me on anything and everything they wished to share about top-level health care. Following that, I got formal nursing training from a facility whose philosophy of care and teaching was equivalent to that of HCHP. Now, I could not possibly remain at Quincy City Hospital. I wished desperately to go back to working as a medical expediter at HCHP, but I could not justify doing so after the two years of nursing education that I had just completed at Newton-Wellesley Hospital School of Nursing. I had to find something that would keep me going forward.

It was in my own backyard.

As a last-ditch effort to recover from the emotional devastation I felt from the "medical care" I had experienced at Quincy Hospital, I called my friend Patty, the woman with whom I shared rides each day during the two years we had attended Newton-Wellesley Hospital School of Nursing together. As I mentioned, Patty was a licensed practical nurse prior to continuing her education to registered nurse status. She was, and continues to be, one of the most conscientious, kind, and intelligent nurses I have ever met.

Telling her of my profound disappointment in the conditions at Quincy Hospital, she invited me over to her house for a cup of tea. She was happily married, had given birth to her first child while we were close to the end of our second and final year at Newton-Wellesley, and would eventually be a mother of three. Pat had the most even-keeled approach to life that I had ever encountered, and we had a wonderful visit and a conversation in which she restored my hope in my own future. As I left her house that afternoon, Patty put her hand on my shoulder and pronounced, "I don't know, Judy, but I just have a feeling that this is going to be your year. Remember this. 1980 will be your year!"

I took two weeks off between jobs while I searched for other sources of nursing employment. I accepted a job at a rehabilitation facility, but my preference for state-of-the-art acute care won out. On March 17, 1980, I accepted a job at South Shore Hospital in Weymouth. It was a great day for *this* Irish-American!

20

1980: As Predicted by Patty

In early 1980, I left my job as an RN at Quincy Hospital and accepted a job at a rehabilitation facility. After the changes in my life, both good and bad, in the previous eight years, I accepted on faith the words of my friend and former nursing schoolmate that 1980 would be *my* year.

It quickly became apparent that my new job was not going to be satisfactory to me, so I left before I wasted much of their time or mine. I then applied for a job at South Shore Hospital. Things didn't initially go smoothly. However, in the meantime, I had decided to once again return to school, this time for my first master's degree. I applied to Bridgewater State College's graduate program in education for a master's degree in counseling.

I was granted an interview at South Shore Hospital for a posted opening for an 11 p.m. to 7 a.m. registered nurse position in the Crisis Intervention Unit (CIU). This was South Shore Hospital's answer to the need for a psychiatric unit. However, as South Shore was an extremely busy medical-surgical hospital, the administrators were loath to dedicate a "whole" unit to psychiatry. Instead, this unit became one of four eight-bed intensive care units (ICUs), with the stipulation that a psychiatric diagnosis alone was not enough for admission to the Unit. A common admission example would be someone who had taken a life-threatening drug overdose as a suicide attempt.

The CIU also served as an overflow unit for the three other ICUs: the Medical Intensive Care Unit, the Surgical Intensive Care Unit, and the Coronary Care Unit.

I liked the idea of getting exposure to a variety of medical, surgical, cardiac, and other acute situations. Additionally, the patient load for each nurse was commonly two, allowing us to devote all our time and attention to what often amounted to the unstable and rapidly changing physical and mental statuses of our patients. Examples of patients the CIU served included: patients in acute detoxification from alcohol through medically monitored withdrawal; patients who had attempted suicide and survived; patients who had been in motor vehicle accidents while under the influence of drugs or alcohol; and even one patient who was caught robbing a pharmacy and swallowed all the narcotics he could grab instead of leaving them behind as he tried to escape. This criminal/patient was under police guard while in the CIU, both because he had stolen the narcotics but also because he had threatened to take a nurse hostage and make his move once he felt that he had recovered from the effects of the drugs he had ingested.

I was hired for the CIU and about to begin my first shift when I was called to the Nursing Personnel office. The director greeted me uncomfortably and said, "Um, Judy, I know I hired you for the CIU, but Carly, another nurse who has already been here a while, hadn't read the new position postings. After Carly heard that I had hired you for the job, she came to complain that she had seniority. I'm sorry, but I'm putting you in as a float nurse until another position comes up in your ivory tower."

This nursing director was a bit of a weirdo, but I *wanted* the job in the Crisis Intervention Unit, although I would hardly classify any intensive care unit in any hospital as an "ivory tower." She had also said something during my initial interview that made me question whether I wanted to work for her, but I found that good jobs were slim pickins' and I had to contain my natural sarcastic retorts if I even wanted a chance at a job that appealed to me.

During my initial interview at South Shore Hospital, she had made her ample body comfortable in the cushioned office chair behind her desk. I sat on a chair opposite her on the other side of her desk and was quite happy with that, as I like my space. In nursing, there are constant violations of personal space, but it comes with the job, so I am even more particular about my private space when it is clearly inappropriate for it to be breached.

After interviewing me from behind her desk for 15 minutes or so, she came to where I was sitting near the corner of the desk and perched herself *on* the corner of the desk with her legs occasionally brushing mine. I was very bothered by it but thought it might be some type of observational test to see how I responded to unwanted body contact. I did not say a word. Next, she pulled a cigarette out of its package and thrust it at me. "Have a cigarette," she offered. I casually answered, "Thank you, but I don't smoke." She gruffly turned to me and demanded, "So I suppose you don't want *me* to smoke because you don't!" With equanimity, I answered, "No, you are welcome to do as you like in your office." The puzzling thing was that she kept looking at me as if I was the inappropriate person in the meeting.

I was incensed, but I did want the job. I had no other choice than to accept the float position, which meant that I would be assigned to different floors and different shifts as needed until another full-time night position came up in CIU. Fortunately, a night shift position opened up in the CIU shortly before I was to start my graduate program at Bridgewater State. Although thought of as "the graveyard shift," my work hours were completely consistent with the hours off I needed to remain available for my graduate program, which started in May of 1980.

Until school began, I worked primarily night shift, although I also sometimes worked weekend days. I loved working the day shift because I got to spend time beside my very favorite person in the unit, Sister Bernadette, a Roman Catholic nun. She was one of the sweetest women I have ever met. Sister Bernadette wore the habit and veil, although a more conservative version than many younger nuns did. (By this time, most Roman Catholic nuns working in the community were not wearing habits at all, but instead modest street clothes.) Her pale blond hair poked out of the sides of the veil, framing her pink cheeks and highlighting her beautiful blue eyes. A long strand of rosary beads encircled her generous waist and hung down her skirt almost to the bottom of her white uniform.

Sister Bernadette was kind to everybody and yet she shocked me one day with a comment about a patient. As a woman of the

cloth, she was devout. She was sweet to the most demanding patients, explaining to the rest of us that their pain might not be visible to us but that they were all suffering.

One Sunday morning, I was working the 7 a.m. to 3 p.m. shift
and Sister Bernadette was among the staff on shift with me. We
clustered around the nurses' station to hear the morning report
from nurses who had worked the night shift so we would know
what to expect for our individual assignments while still being able
to assist with other more acutely ill patients as needed.

During the report, we were all startled by the sound of a man
yelling harshly, but not as if he were in pain. All of us turned to look
at the patient in room CIU 6, who was sitting up in a hospital chair
surrounded by his family. What had caught our attention was his
raised voice as he screamed at them, "I am in this damn hospital
because *you* put me here! It's the fault of all of you that I keep trying
to kill myself!" We recognized him instantly as a "frequent flyer,"
one of the extremely rare patients who had had multiple admissions
to the CIU for attempting to commit suicide.

As nurses, all of us, including Sister Bernadette, had a great
deal of compassion for patients who suffered such deep depression that they felt that they could not go on living. We had seen
so many patients who had been brought in and not survived, and
many others who had attempted suicide and recovered enough to
be discharged to a longer-term-care psychiatric hospital.

I remember one woman who attempted suicide because her
husband had left her for another woman. She was hospitalized
in CIU and swore to all the staff that she was profoundly embarrassed by what she had done. She said that she had believed that
when her husband heard that she was hospitalized for a suicide
attempt he would come back to her. However, in the week that she
was in CIU, he never even visited her. The patient convinced the
nursing staff and her psychiatrist that she was absolutely not suicidal, only humiliated. She was so convincing that her psychiatrist
did not pressure her to be admitted to a psychiatric facility for a
short-term stay before releasing her to home. She went home. And
killed herself.

This older male patient was just the opposite. He professed to
be suicidal any time anyone in his family made him angry, and he
was always angry. He used a variety of methods that convinced his

family that *this* time he was "really suicidal." But when they would come in to visit him, he spent the entire time berating them and screaming that it was entirely their fault.

I was standing next to Sister Bernadette when we all realized that this was the same man who was admitted about once every six weeks for the same type of event. As she and I listened to the morning report, we could hear him screaming over all of the talking, and buzzers, and beepers, and respirators, and other noise-making equipment in the unit.

Sister Bernadette leaned close to me and whispered, "Dear God. The next time he attempts suicide, please let him succeed." I spun around and looked at her. I quietly said, "Sister, we are both Catholic! We are not supposed to encourage suicide!" She thoughtfully said to me, "The way he is torturing his family is a far greater sin." She looked both gray and grave as she said this to me. I gave her a hug and whispered that I understood how she felt. However, it was our duty as registered nurses to save lives at all costs, and it was also our obligation as Catholics.

Because of the changes brought about by the Second Ecumenical Council, Vatican II, Sister Bernadette was able to work as a nurse in a secular establishment and did not have to be accompanied by another nun when outside of the convent. Most nuns during Sister Bernadette's era lived out in the community, in contrast to the convents that had housed almost all nuns prior to Vatican II. As well, her short veil and knee-length uniform were radically different from the voluminous garments and elaborate headwear worn by nuns prior to Vatican II.

Sister Bernadette was very encouraging about me being in the master's program in counseling and had often praised me for times she'd overheard me having concerned and lengthy conversations with our patients. She knew I was as deeply interested in helping other people with their emotional issues as I was with their physical problems. She would, without telling me, show my professional written assessments of patients' mental health concerns to the doctors and to the nursing supervisors, where relevant. She believed that my notes would enhance the care patients were receiving while they were in the CIU and thereafter. Because of her welcome interventions (she could do no wrong as far as I was concerned), the psychiatrists often asked me to share my observations with them about their CIU patients. I learned a great deal from Sister Bernadette, especially how much a kind word can do for someone in distress, whether patient or private citizen.

Sister Bernadette was determined to change the dynamic between this chronically angry man and family who became terrified (and resentful) each new time he was admitted for suicidal ideation. She spent hours, including staying after her own shift ended, sitting with him and his family in the conference room. She ultimately helped all of them to negotiate a way that he could communicate to his family when he felt sick, angry, or uncomfortable. She helped them to see that it was frustration he was experiencing and not a desire to bring about his own death that made for such poor family communication patterns.

21

The Maxwell Library

Having worked in health care for so many years, I had finally determined that my long-term goal was to work in some capacity that involved close contact with clients and teaching. Thus, I was back at Bridgewater State, taking classes primarily in my favorite building—the Maxwell Library.

Because I hadn't yet taken an introductory course in statistics, I signed up to start in May of 1980 so I could complete this prerequisite for the MEd program, which would begin two months later.

My life was finally falling into place. I had vacated the apartment in Braintree I had occupied for seven years and rented a studio apartment on Summer Street in Bridgewater, just a few minutes' walking distance to my anticipated classes. I was now living just off-campus, working the night shift at South Shore Hospital, and driving down Route 18 just after my shift ended. I would stop for a cup of Dunkin' Donuts coffee to tide me over and arrive in Bridgewater just in time for my morning statistics classes.

After statistics ended at 1:00 p.m., I would go back to my apartment, have a light lunch, and try desperately to sleep for at least four to six hours before I left again at 10 p.m. to return to the night shift. However, I had (and still have) a sleep disorder that renders me unable to doze off when I have plenty of time to sleep. Instead, I lie awake for hours, failing dismally at falling asleep and only dozing off within an hour or so of the time I have to get up for work. It was becoming very frustrating to get into bed after class and lie there counting sheep, counting dust mites, getting out of bed and counting all of my shoes, and finally calling my sister Kathy to talk about my first niece Katie, who had been born just months before.

After a few weeks of wasting the afternoon trying unsuccessfully to sleep, I decided to stay up after class and try sleeping instead from 6 p.m. to 10 p.m. and then get up and get ready for work. It *had* to be more sleep than I was currently getting.

That left my afternoons after statistics class free. Where else would I rather spend them than in a library? What a wonderful coincidence that my class was already in the library! I had a very short commute to the stacks of books available to borrow for my elucidation and entertainment.

Soon I noticed that I seemed to get the same librarian over and over, and he was very accommodating, offering further suggestions to my reading choices. I was very impressed with how well read he was and with his conversational skills. His personality was also impressive.

As he checked out books for me, he said, "Here you are, Judy. I hope you enjoy these." I was flattered that he had inserted my name in the exchange, and I put my hand out for a shake, saying, "Pleased to meet you—?", hoping my implicit question mark at the end would encourage him to tell me his name. He laughed and said, "I am Jeremiah. I have been the Acquisitions Librarian here for the past five years, and I work a lot with the graduate students."

Excitedly, I remarked, "I am going to start the master of education program in counseling in July. I am at Bridgewater now taking statistics as a prerequisite." We left the conversation at that, and I went back to my apartment. On my next foray to the library, he walked over to the desk just as I was about to check out my books and leave. "Hi, Judy," he said, "You must spend a lot of time reading since you are taking out books and returning them every couple of days."

I commented that I was a full-time registered nurse, and so I had to fit my reading into the hours before and after my shift. The conversation continued about my job, and then he slid into the discussion a casual invitation to coffee—right then. I agreed, and we went off-campus during his break.

I was sizing him up as he did me while we had our coffee. He was single. Check. He was well-educated. Check. He was easy on the eye. (Shallow, but check). But his mannerisms were somewhat stiff. I felt as if he were in a century-old play. On balance, he was a very nice guy, but my hackles were up a bit.

I left for work in the Crisis Intervention Unit at South Shore Hospital each evening about ten p.m., giving me time to stop at Dunkin' Donuts (again) for a fresh cup of coffee to fuel me for the shift ahead. One afternoon, he asked if we could have a light dinner early, go for a walk through the picturesque Bridgewater Town Common, and then walk around some of the local neighborhoods with their grand houses. He assured me that I would get to work on time. I agreed and met him for dinner in a local diner.

Conversation was still a bit awkward, but I decided to give him a chance. We finished eating and started our walk around the center. Our conversation was a bit concerning, just enough to toss out warning signs.

Suddenly, a street sweeper came by with its flashing lights and slow pace. He suddenly leaped in front of the street sweeper, yelling, "*Flame throwers! Flame throwers!*" The street sweeper swerved and just missed hitting him. Upon his outburst, I froze on the sidewalk. And then I got upset. I didn't know whether his was a post-traumatic stress reaction to combat. I had no idea even if he had been in the service. Most curious was that as soon as he shouted out, he looked toward me and ran back to my side, acting as if nothing unusual had occurred.

Working in a psychiatric unit, I had dealt with people reliving their previous traumas. But I had never seen anyone who had an episode that lasted a minute or two and then completely recovered. He put his arm casually on my shoulder and asked, "Shall we continue our walk?"

"No," I said. "I have to go in to work early tonight." In the back of my mind was that I had been married to a man with severe mental health issues who never sought treatment. I was not going to volunteer to be in a relationship where the partner used high drama for attention or refused mental health care for past trauma.

That wasn't quite the end of it. He wanted to come back to my apartment, and I abruptly said, "I am already in my uniform. I am just walking back to get my car. You don't need to go with me." He pulled me onto a bench on the town common. I was expecting some sort of minimization or apology for the dramatic and somewhat alarming behavior. Instead, he looked into my face and murmured, "You have skin like alabaster and hair like flax." I wanted to say, "And I can run like a fleet-footed deer!" Instead, off I went but not until I kindly said to him, "Thank you, Jeremiah, for your time and attention, but we are very much different from each other."

He looked despondent as I jumped in my car and headed post-haste up Route 18 to South Shore Hospital and the respite of my hectic job. But the Dunkin' coffee soothed me on the way.

For the next few weeks, I primarily was at work, in class, or in my apartment. I avoided the library and bought whatever books I wanted to read. But the day had to come eventually when I would be required to check out and return assigned books and readings from the Maxwell Library. I assumed that Jeremiah would still be there and found soon after that he was. When I brought the books that I needed to his desk he was courteous but distant with me. I breathed a sigh of relief. It seemed that there were no hard feelings about our disastrous date, and it was rather obvious that I was not interested in a second dinner together.

I was tired of spending so much time in my apartment when I was not at work due to my desire to avoid Jeremiah, and I decided that it was time to enjoy the great weather as my statistics course was coming to an end.

The beautiful summer weather induced me to rush home from work each day, change out of my uniform into street clothes if I had time, and sit on the steps of the Maxwell Library, right outside the classroom where my Introduction to Counseling course would be held. I was eagerly looking forward to formally beginning the master's program. As I sashayed around the classroom area, I met the man who would be my first professor in the program, Professor Hammersmith. He was carrying with him an *Introduction to Counseling* text, so at first I thought he might be an incoming student. Since it was just before the July 4 holiday, I assumed that if he were also a student he was getting comfortable with the environment before our program began on July 6. We started to talk, and he told me that he was, in fact, the director of the counseling program. I was thrilled! This was *so* much better than when I had been a brand-new undergraduate at Bridgewater State College in 1972, and on the first day of class, our history professor threw the whole class out of the room because we had not come prepared with pens and notebooks and our text as *real* college students should do. No, Professor Hammersmith was nothing like Professor Wolf.

We chatted for a while about the program and looked forward to seeing each other in class.

Thus, on the morning of July 6, I went directly from the night shift at South Shore Hospital to the Maxwell Library. The weather was seasonably hot, and I was still in my nursing uniform. I was so excited to begin the program that I didn't even notice the temperature. Instead, I watched people as they approached the building, wondering which ones were to be in the same class with me and Professor Hammersmith. I got up to walk around the outside of the building and noticed the cars coming onto campus. One stood out: a white Pontiac Firebird with a blue racing stripe. I'm not normally interested in cars, but this particular one was striking. I saw the driver park the car in the gymnasium parking lot across from Maxwell Library, and he began to approach "my" building. The man had a swarthy appearance, dark wavy hair, and appeared to be a gym rat. "Not my type" was my immediate thought. He walked past me, nodding his head but not saying anything. Yet when I came into the classroom and sat in the front of the room, I noticed him sitting in the back corner, looking somewhat sullen. Now, looking back, I question my own ability to assess first appearances.

Class soon began, and Professor Hammersmith came in smiling and seemingly very happy to see that the counseling program was starting off with a full complement. He talked a bit about himself and then directed us to go around the room, starting with the back row, and introduce ourselves. He suggested that we say where we lived, what we did with the time that we were not in school (remaining vague on purpose), and that, following introductions, we take an immediate break to interact with others.

One by one, the students in the back row spoke about themselves, taking varying amounts of time, depending on how much they wanted to divulge on the first day. After the third student spoke, the man in the fourth row, last seat, pleasantly said, "Hi, my name is Miles. I am a teacher in Weymouth, and I am here because I eventually want to be a high school guidance counselor." Last row, last seat said abruptly, "Rich, Weymouth, teacher." I was a little stunned.

I am rather loquacious normally, but I decided uncharac-
teristically to follow the last speaker's lead. I said, "Judy, I live in
Bridgewater, and I am a registered nurse in Weymouth." I turned
and smiled at the two Weymouth teachers who had just introduced
themselves. After a short lecture, we had a break. I saw the two
Weymouth guys chatting, and I went over to speak with them. The
seemingly sullen Firebird driver smiled easily at me and was a bit
friendlier. Miles led the conversation among we three Weymou-
thites, and soon we were asked to return to our seats so that class
could begin. I took notes as Professor Hammersmith (who asked
us just to call him "Bob") lectured. But I couldn't get Rich off my
mind. As class ended, people gravitated toward others for further
conversation. I turned in Rich's direction and saw him meandering
toward me. Miles joined us in the conversation and continued to
make small talk, but I noticed that Rich was directing much of his
conversation toward me, as I was to him. Miles announced that he
had to leave, and Rich and I walked out together. I started to walk
to my nearby apartment and Rich asked if I minded if he walked
with me. I voiced no objections whatsoever. I found myself inviting
him into the apartment and offered to make us sandwiches. This
was definitely not like me! As an aside, I teased my three daughters
for many years whenever they would ask me how I met Daddy. I'd
answer kiddingly, "He said, 'I'm Rich,' and I said, 'Then I'm available!'" Sad to say, they believed that to be true for decades. I finally
realized that I had set a very bad example for them with my joke
and clarified to them that, actually, we met because we found ourselves immediately to be comfortable and compatible together. (I
think they liked the other story better.)

That first day, I happened to make sandwiches on Syrian
bread. He immediately said, "I am Lebanese! Wait until I get you
real Syrian bread from the South End of Boston. That's where I was
born!" He explained that all of his relatives were Lebanese and Syrian, which were technically the same ethnicity since Syria was once
a part of Lebanon.

What interested me most was that he was planning a future
event already—getting me Syrian bread. We talked a lot about food
during that lunch, obviously to us because it was a driving interest
we shared. We continued to learn more and more about each other
in that one afternoon, and he told me that he went lobstering with

his friends. I exclaimed, "I love lobster!" He answered enthusiastically, "Stay with me and I will get you lobster for the rest of your life." I was aghast but now hungrier. The irony is that he never did get me a lobster directly from the ocean: we spent so much time together that it precluded lobstering with his friends ever again. But he has always gotten fresh lobster meat for me from Wood's Seafood in Plymouth, Massachusetts, and gets overstuffed lobster sandwiches from Green Harbor Seafood in Marshfield even now.

We were both obviously smitten from the start, but I kept hearing in my head my mother's warning, too late the first time around, that if you "marry in haste, you repent at leisure."

I tried to hold back my enthusiasm about a long-term relationship and started looking for signs to still my beating heart. After lunch, we spent time walking around Bridgewater Common until I had to get a few hours' sleep and then head back to South Shore Hospital.

That next morning, I sat on the steps of Maxwell again, waiting for the white Firebird to glide by. In a short time, I spotted the car but sat on the steps willing myself to be patient and assess his response to me before I just ran over to him. As he drove by, he looked at me again with the same expression he had had on our initial meeting: somewhat reserved and with a casual smile. I thought, "Oh, I guess he also thinks we might both have been a little too enthusiastic yesterday about a possible relationship." I watched him park his car and then jog across the street and sit down beside me on the steps where we talked, both smiling broadly, till we had to go into class. At 1 p.m., we casually agreed to have lunch again in my apartment. I suggested that he move the car to my parking lot so he wouldn't have to return later to retrieve it. I walked to the car with him, and my heart fell. I noticed on the back seat an orange Speedo bathing suit. Immediately I sucked in a breath and concluded that this guy must be a player! I mentioned the bathing suit and he said words that made me grin broadly. He explained, "I have four older aunts that live together, and they have a pool about five minutes from my family's home. We always go swimming there. It's great because the aunts also wait hand and foot on my brother and me. You should come with us!"

My head started to spin. "Hmm," I thought, "I guess this is on!"

And on Friday of that week, I walked over to meet Rich in the parking lot at the beginning of the school day. He immediately said, "I have a plan. I hope you will like it. I am invited to a party tomorrow afternoon. I know that you have to work tomorrow night, but I was thinking that I could drive you to work tonight and return you home so you can sleep for a few hours. I will come by at 5 p.m. so that you can come to the party with me. If you bring your nursing uniform with you, we can enjoy the party for a few hours, and then I will drive you in for your 11 p.m. shift." I was thoroughly impressed with his planning, but I do admit that I asked myself sincerely, "Is this another rush? The last one when I worked at Grants didn't work out so well."

And yet I was so astonished by his very careful planning of all the logistics, including beginning and ending work hours, getting me to and from the party, thinking about me bringing my uniform so that I wouldn't be late for work, and then ferrying me home after my 11 p.m. to 7 a.m. shift so that I could sleep again after the busy night.

I scrutinized his expression to see if he was playing me. But he had a beaming smile, and he became almost breathless with excitement when I said "Yes."

Rich and I became an established couple rapidly. A concern early on was that we had decided to live together, but it had to be someplace that accommodated both of our jobs as well. It was hard to find affordable housing in Weymouth, and we both worked in the town. We started contacting realtors and reading newspaper advertisements for available apartments, but nothing fit our needs.

Sister Bernadette was a dear woman, and I benefitted greatly from working with her. One way that she helped me had to do with my newly forming relationship with the man who began as my schoolmate and then became my husband and ultimately the father of our three daughters. Sister Bernadette actually helped us to cohabit without benefit of marriage! Again, something highly discouraged by devout Catholics, but she had met my new boyfriend/classmate Rich and knew instinctively that something good was here to stay. Sister Bernadette found us our first apartment!

Sister was a big booster of the time and interest that I put into my studies. She was also one of the first people I told about my soon-to-be husband Rich (as we had gotten officially engaged within two months of meeting each other).

A conundrum that Rich and I had was that he was still living at his family home in Weymouth, and I had a studio apartment just off the campus in Bridgewater. We spent a fair amount of time at my apartment when we were not in classes or working. We planned an April 1981 wedding and decided that we definitely wanted our own apartment before that time. But apartments were hard to come by that were convenient for our Weymouth jobs, our Bridgewater classes, and our opposite working schedules. I was still working full-time on the "midnight" shift and Rich was working days teaching and coaching. We needed to find something affordable and roomier than a studio apartment that was along Route 18 between the two towns where we spent most of our time.

I had confided our dilemma to a co-worker Bill, also a registered nurse in the CIU. He answered that Sister Bernadette had just asked on morning rounds a couple of weeks before if any of the nurses knew anyone looking for an apartment. Sister Bernadette had a friend vacating an apartment in a small complex in Abington, the town next to Weymouth. The apartment was within walking distance from Route 18. Bill passed the information on to me during our night shift. He said to me, "Sister Bernadette is working in the morning. Why don't you ask her when she comes in if it is still available?"

I was so excited that I was counting the minutes until she arrived. Bill and I had a very friendly relationship, often teasing one another, but we had each other's backs when things went haywire on our night shift, especially when we were short-staffed. Fortunately, this had been a relatively calm night. Sister Bernadette got into work early and came over to the desk before shift report was about to begin. Bill immediately said, "Sister, Judy has something she wants to ask you." She turned to me with her angelic face, anticipating my question. I said quickly and anxiously, "Is your friend's apartment in Abington still available? I am looking for an apartment immediately and the location is absolutely ideal!"

She smiled at me and said, "I believe so. If you can wait until report is over, I will call her and find out."

With twinkling eyes, Bill looked at her and solemnly said, "Um, Sister Bernadette. Why would you, a Catholic nun, provide a refuge for sin for Judy?" Sister Bernadette at first looked flustered and turned to me. I didn't know whether to hit Bill or laugh but I turned scarlet and turned back to Sister Bernadette. Bill didn't give either of us a chance to say anything as he continued on, "Judy wants the apartment to cohabit with her boyfriend. Isn't that a sin?" I could feel my fists ball up. Sister and Bill began to laugh and she answered, "Bill, you know that Judy and Rich are engaged to be married in a couple of months. I think it's fine for them to get their apartment ready for their marriage." I looked in her direction, and she winked at me. I gave her a hug, still not knowing if the apartment was available or not. And then I kicked Bill under the nurses' desk. Not surprisingly, he said, "Sister, she just kicked me!" Taking my side again, my dear angelic Sister Bernadette answered, "I would have too, if I were Judy!"

As it turned out, the apartment was available, affordable, and beautiful. Rich's only sibling, his brother Tom, generously furnished it for us. The gods were smiling on us, and we eagerly anticipated the wedding.

Admittedly, we had a whirlwind courtship and marriage. We met in July, became engaged two months later, married in March of 1981, and had our first child Kara in November of 1981. In the meantime, we moved to our first house in Marshfield. We graduated with our master's degrees in counseling from Bridgewater State College in May of 1982, along with my sister Kathy, who had earned a master's degree in library science. My family had a party for us at their Duxbury home, where there was even more to celebrate. My ten-years-younger sister Christine had graduated the very same day from Sacred Heart High School in Kingston. Our baby daughter Kara celebrated with us.

The one sour note was that the weather predictions for the day were dismal. Torrential rain was predicted. Sure enough, as the Bridgewater State College undergraduate and graduate degree candidates took their seats under the tent, ominous thunder sounded. Nonetheless, the president of the college optimistically started the welcoming speech. The rain suddenly burst from the clouds, and it meant business. No one could pay attention to the opening remarks of speakers as we couldn't hear over the thunder. I glanced up at the roof of the tent and noticed that water was rapidly pooling, causing a significant water-filled depression right above our heads.

Suddenly, a man jumped up on the stage, grabbed the microphone away from the speaker, and announced alarmingly, "The Army Corps of Engineers has determined that this tent will collapse within 20 minutes. *Evacuate* immediately!"

We got out! Avoiding a looming tragedy was the primary concern, and we were all safe, but we stubbornly wanted our degrees in hand before we left the campus. If there had been a news helicopter flying overhead, they would have viewed the chaotic scene of hundreds of people running all over campus in now-soaked graduation gowns and wilted graduation caps calling out, "Where's my diploma? Where's my diploma?"

In the chaos, a few administrators made rapid arrangements to take *all* of the previously alphabetically sorted documents to the Campus Center. Graduates were directed there to get their degrees and leave campus as soon as possible. It worked. We were soaked but generally happy.

The widespread sentiment was that the undergraduates were the most betrayed by nature. A significant number of those who had earned bachelor's degrees were the first in their families to do so. For most, this was the only formal degree they would earn. Family members in the audience were bitterly disappointed at not watching their groundbreaking graduate shake hands with the college president with their right hand as they accepted their degree with the left hand. Unfortunately, such is life. We all had truly completed our mission to earn our specified degrees. Parties were still on!

It was back to work a couple of days later. We were no longer the stars of the day. Rich and I, however, returned happily to our family's needs.

Our next objective was to buy a house. We purchased what we could afford: a tiny, converted cottage in Marshfield. Lindsey, baby girl number two, was born on July 6, 1983. By coincidence, that was also the anniversary of the date that Rich and I met at Bridgewater.

In December of 1984, our third daughter Courtney was born. We moved into our first newly built Marshfield home to accommodate the latest increase in family size.

Over the next few decades, there were job changes and promotions. Rich became a guidance counselor at Silver Lake Regional High School; by the time of his retirement in 2013, he was principal.

When the high school was rebuilt, the auditorium was named in his honor—the Richard J. Kelley, Jr. Auditorium.

Our children and grandchildren have all spent time dancing in the empty auditorium with Grampy and Mimi proudly looking on.

In the meantime, I accumulated degrees, adjunct faculty jobs as a college professor, and ultimately full-time jobs in my finally-decided-upon field. I've taught in numerous schools, including Quincy College and College of the Holy Cross. For 23 years, I've been a professor of sociology, criminal justice, and also health sciences. We have finally both retired and surprisingly stayed in our Duxbury home into which we moved in 2003.

In the intervening years, life went on. And sometimes it didn't. We, like most people, have had the bad fortune of losing many loved ones to both premature death and deaths anticipated from long-term chronic illnesses. My nursing training facilitated the provision of both informal and formal care for family members who have suffered and then recovered, as well as those who have died in our 40 years together.

My nursing training has stood me (and others) in good stead as we have all negotiated both anticipated and unexpected life events.

Of all of the years that I worked in nursing, a number of colleagues have either mentored me, supported me, or made the job a joy, even in the most unpleasant circumstances. Sister Bernadette is on that list, as are a few special others, but the one unforgettable nurse who changed my life the most was Melody.

22

Melody

When I was 30 years old, Rich and I had our third and final child, Courtney. Prior to her birth, I was once again planning on attending another graduate school—Boston University School of Public Health—for a second master's degree and was struggling to juggle our family schedules. Rich and I had made the decision that I stay at home during the day with the kids until *they* were all in school. I needed a part-time job that would accommodate our children, Rich's work schedule, and my studies. After a year and a half foray into psychiatric nursing at Westwood Lodge Hospital and then its sister facility, Pembroke Hospital, I found myself returning to work part-time at South Shore Hospital, once again as a float nurse on the evening shift.

The advantage of the "float" position was that I got to experience different hospital units to see what other opportunities I might have in the years that I expected to continue working at South Shore Hospital. I finally was offered exactly what I had decided that I wanted next: a position in the maternity unit doing labor and delivery nursing, and post-partum care. But there was a hitch: I had just given birth to Courtney when I got the call from South Shore that a full-time day position was mine to claim. I was at first excited and then indecisive, and finally determined that I could not give up caring for my own three children during the day to take care of other people during their labor and delivery experiences. What a dilemma. But I just did not want to leave my own precious three little ones.

When I had initially gone to South Shore Hospital in March of 1980 for the newly available position in the CIU, the offer was rescinded in favor of a more senior nurse who fought for it after I was hired. I agreed to wait for the next CIU position to open up while I worked as a float nurse and was often sent to a medical surgical unit that was chronically short of help on the evening shift. Here I met the most unforgettable woman of my life, a licensed practical nurse with as much compassion as her rollicking sense of humor. She was Melody, and I came to adore her as much as anyone with whom I have ever had the pleasure of working.

Melody Monteiro was one of the funniest, kindest, most compassionate, and loving women I have ever known. I started at South Shore Hospital as a registered nurse in March of 1980, initially full-time but later per diem. While I worked per diem in the early 1980s, I "floated" to nearly every unit in the hospital on all three shifts. The Pratt Building housed the medical-surgical unit where I first met Licensed Practical Nurse Melody.

I now limited my work schedules to evenings and weekends while Rich and I were juggling our young family. We owned only one car. Living in Marshfield, Rich often had to pack up the kids to bring me to work for a 3 p.m. to 11 p.m. shift and then wake up our three little daughters at 10:00 p.m. to retrieve me from work, with a tired Daddy driving.

On unit Four South, I first met Melody, an uproariously funny, outrageous, and voluptuous woman who was clearly loved by everyone who had ever met her. She swore, she was loud, and she loved her food—telling tales of stopping by Marshfield Famous Pizza, often at 1 a.m. after a delayed departure from her 3 p.m. to 11 p.m. shift. She bragged of getting herself a large submarine sandwich, going home to Rexhame, (a village of Marshfield), and consuming the entire snack prior to climbing into bed with her sleeping husband. Her young children, Jonathan and Anna, were obviously used to Melody's raucous entry and her collapse into the kitchen chair where she relished her post-work treat. If the kids woke up, she comforted them, gave them a glass of water (or a milkshake), and then put them back to bed.

I had only been a working mother of three as a per diem nurse for a short time on the 3 to 11 p.m. shift, but my family was suffering from exhaustion. Rich got home from his teaching job just in time to drive me to work, and then was in charge of our three kids. When they should have been home playing, eating supper, bathing, and going to bed for the night because of our car situation, he had to wake them up and pack them all up at 10 p.m. to pick me up when my shifts ended.

I was bemoaning the situation at work one evening when Melody loudly called across the nurses' station, "You live in Marshfield too, right?" I answered, "Yes," and she generously said, "I can take you home whenever we work together, as long as you don't mind stopping off for a very late snack. You can take it home to eat it like I do. I don't think Famous Pizza would let us dine in after midnight!"

I was reluctant to accept the ride since I had only recently met her, and I was hesitant to inconvenience her. She scoffed, "Don't be silly. We're going the same way, and this way your husband won't have to wake your kids out of a sound sleep to pick you up."

Melody overcame my discomfort at accepting her help with her perceptive appeal for the "good of your kids." I gratefully accepted her offer. Riding home, I was exposed to Melody's rapier wit, her infectious laughter, and her incredibly kind smile. She was always laughing or at the very least smiling broadly and sincerely, no matter the situation.

As nurses, we busted our behinds. The evening shifts often flew by due to the heavy workload and limited staff. A few of us working with Melody and her usual team were floats assigned on arriving at work to a unit that was smaller than the sufficient number of staff to cover the shift. As it turned out, Melody's floor was often left short—I believe this was largely because Melody would accept the most burdensome patient load without complaint.

The more I worked with Melody, the more delighted I became with my new friend. Melody did not have an inhibited bone in her body. We were on break with a room full of staff attracted to the comfortable sofa and chairs in the lounge. As we all sat enjoying coffee or cold drinks, Melody yelled out, "Hey, everybody, how do you like my yellow polyester pants? It's all the uniform store had in my size 18."

The pants *weren't* exactly yellow, but they weren't quite white either. Everyone laughed except me. I cringed with embarrassment that Melody so openly threw out her clothing size for common knowledge. I was far shorter than Melody and wore the same size that she did and had never ever imagined that, unlike me, she would not have considered her body mass to be an object of derision. In my estimation, the situation worsened when she bit into a jelly donut as she laughed about her own work wardrobe and a blob of strawberry jelly fell onto her pants.

The usual response when staff found themselves in soiled clothing, typically from stains related to caring for patients with leaky body bits, was to borrow a pair of standard scrub pants from the operating room and continue with the shift. Melody, being Melody, simply dabbed at the jelly stain and said, "Wow, now I'm like a traffic light. My size 18 pants are yellow *and* red!" I tittered as she guffawed.

I realized early on that working alongside Melody was a rare event that I came to anticipate with the knowledge that she'd work me hard but keep me laughing even harder.

I also realized that Melody's absolutely outrageous sense of humor was appreciated by even the most unlikely hospital employees—the surgeons. Melody could and did say whatever came into her head to anybody and everybody. As kind as she was to her patients, Melody was joyfully careless with her words to the most pompous of doctors and other individuals who possessed overly large egos.

We took our supper break together one evening and were walking with the heavy flow of hungry employees traversing the right side of the corridor while those sated by the hospital supper passed us by in the other direction returning to their assigned units. A group of three doctors approached Melody and me. As they got closer, and then elbow-to-elbow with us, none of us acknowledged the others. It was all employees either hurrying to dinner or back to work. As Dr. McCarville, an older, distinguished physician, passed Melody, I watched in horror as she quickly spun around, grabbed a significant chunk of his rear end, and laughed.

"I'm going to get fired, I'm going to get fired," played in my head as I quickly realized that Melody had goosed the great and mighty orthopedic physician. I burned with borrowed humiliation while Melody shrieked with laughter at her own prank. I glanced back in horror, expecting Dr. McCarville to erupt in a rage at her. Melody wore not a look of shame, but one of great mirth. Dr. McCarville glanced at her, turned to walk away, and burst loudly into a cacophonous rendition of "A pretty girl . . . is like a melody!" Everyone loved her.

Melody could do no wrong. And yet she did . . . and so often in my presence. None of the other hundred or so travelers in the tight hallway even acknowledged the event, which was historic in my mind. I finally stuttered, "Melody!! Why did you do that??? You could have gotten fired!" She offered me no excuses but continued on her way to a luscious dinner of hospital-cooked macaroni and cheese. With dessert.

Melody was a lovely woman, but she did not tolerate unkindness from others. The epitome of crassness toward patients and staff was Dr. Gronberg, a neurologist. I had known him for years, as he worked simultaneously at roughly five hospitals. His first order of business on getting to a nursing unit was to go to the desk and loudly call his accountant. Every time, at every hospital! And what we could all clearly hear him ask was which checks had come in. When I made employment changes in nursing, he would always be where I was currently working. Always in the shabby black suit. He carried around a stack of index cards with the names of his patients in each hospital. He appeared on the nursing units at random hours, around the clock, interrupting staff who were otherwise occupied, demanding, "I need two nurses right this minute. I am going to do a lumbar puncture."

I was assisting him with the procedure commonly known as a "spinal tap" one afternoon at Quincy Hospital, and his patient was a humble and gentle but very obese man in his 30s. Dr. Gronberg, significantly older, was obese as well. Dr. Gronberg took his position at the bedside and demanded that I stand across from him. He said to me about the patient, "Grab his fat neck and pull it down toward his knees as hard as you can. With your other arm, pull the back of his knees up toward his fat head. I need as much expansion of the spinal space as I can get."

I was appalled by the way he referred to the patient, as this doctor was no "slim jim" himself. The young man was nearly in tears. As Dr. Gronberg berated him while having difficulty locating a good point of entry for the spinal needle, he insulted the patient further, and demanded that I try "*harder*" to pull the poor man's head and knees within two feet of each other.

Suddenly, Dr. Gronberg noticed that there was a Whitman's

sampler chocolate assortment at the patient's bedside. He stopped the procedure, reached over to the table, opened the candy, and grabbed a handful without even asking permission. As Dr. Gronberg went back to the procedure, he filled his gaping mouth with chocolates. As he chewed, saliva dripped down onto his chin. And yet he still continued to yell at the patient for "being too fat to make this procedure work safely."

As enraged as I was, I bit my tongue for the sake of the already upset patient. I chalked it up as yet another of Dr. Gronberg's patient-provider interaction horrors. I could have written a second list of incidents related to his lack of finesse with nursing staff. So many nurses in so many hospitals dreaded seeing the portly man in the shabby black suit showing up and ordering around everyone whom he deemed to be subject to his demands. In one instance, however, Melody brought justice to all of us: nurses, nursing assistants, supervisors, patients, and best of all, to Dr. Gronberg himself.

That evening I was fortunate enough to have been assigned to work on Melody's floor again. I always thanked my lucky stars when I got that plum assignment. Everybody in the hospital knew and loved Melody—and *I* got to work with her.

About 8 p.m., Dr. Gronberg arrived, called his accountant, and got his report of payments for services provided. Satisfied, he turned his attention to the task at hand. Without preamble, he grabbed both Melody and me and said, "*Now!* I have an LP [lumbar puncture] with Danforth." Melody smiled and said to him, "I assume that you are requesting our assistance with *Mrs.* Danforth." He muttered, "Yeah. *Now!*" I was angry but followed Melody into the patient's room. A frail, frightened elderly woman turned pale when she saw him. She became terrified when he announced abruptly that he had to stick a long needle into her spine and that we were going to force her into the necessary position. I looked angrily at Melody, and she winked at me. I calmed down, as Melody suddenly hugged the old woman and said, "Hey, beautiful girl. I am going to ask you to lie on your side. We'll help you. Once you are on your side, I am going to give you a big hug! I'm going to hug you around your neck and under your knees. If you can, please pull your knees up toward your head, and Judy and I will hold you." The elderly woman whimpered at Melody, but Melody continued to smile and gently reassure the timid patient.

Dr. Gronberg leaned over to start disinfection of the area for the procedure, but the patient was so petite that Dr. Gronberg was unable to bend over far enough to be comfortable while he proceeded. He looked at me and yelled, "Grab me that chair and pull it over here." It was a desk chair, cushioned and on wheels. I wasn't sure why it was in the patient room, where it was not part of the usual setup, but I grimaced and pushed it toward him. Dr. Gronberg grabbed the chair hurriedly and as he tried to plop his overly generous posterior onto the seat, the wheels skittered, and he fell off the edge of the chair. Those of us assisting, except Melody, all politely coughed to suppress our mirth and pretended that we hadn't really noticed what had happened. *Not* Melody! She roared with laughter at him and yelled, "Hey, Dr. Gronberg, look at you rolling all around the floor on your fat ass! You must feel like a total idiot!"

He looked up at her with fury! I was never so satisfied in my life. And yet to look at Melody's expression, she didn't act as if she was being hurtful. She simply looked delighted. She leaned over Dr. Gronberg and extended a hand. As he reached up, she pulled her helping hand away and yelled, "*Got ya!*" I was in agony trying to choke back my hysteria! The poor patient was upset by the commotion, and Melody turned away from the doctor, who was trying to regain a respectable position, and attended instead to the old woman. Melody hugged her and said, "Sweetie, I'm going to stay with you and bathe you and get you comfortable for sleep. Dr. Gronberg will come back another time." Angry yet chagrined, he left.

So many times when I worked with Melody, what kept playing through my head was the phrase, "I'm going to get fired. I'm going to get fired." I was Melody's best audience, encouraging her unpredictably funny yet often inappropriate behavior. Yet anyone who turned their head in Melody's direction upon being surprised by what came out of her mouth would smile, witnessing her beautiful and sincere expression even when she was "teasing," as she put it. But she always made her point.

Months later, I was once again floated to Melody's floor to take the place of an absent registered nurse. Together we provided evening care for patients in rooms on one side of the unit. As we checked on another elderly patient, this one scheduled to be transferred by ambulance for a cancer treatment the next day, we found her unwell. The transfer was to be just for the day as at that time Brockton Hospital had equipment that South Shore Hospital did not have for the relatively new and complex procedure the patient needed.

The woman tearfully told us that she was just not up to the transfer the next day and begged us to call Brockton Hospital to cancel. We contacted her South Shore attending physician and he approved the cancellation. He requested that we notify the treating oncologist at Brockton Hospital. We tried repeatedly to do so, but for some inexplicable reason the telephone operator at Brockton refused to believe that we were calling from South Shore Hospital. It made no sense whatsoever. We told her the patient's name, her local doctor's name, and the name of the treating doctor at Brockton. And yet the switchboard operator was adamant that we were pranking her. It was odd. We asked her reasonably to call back South Shore herself and ask for the ward secretary on our unit to confirm the information that we were trying to convey. She refused. We were flummoxed trying to figure out how we would be able to leave word that the patient would not be arriving for the scheduled appointment the next day.

We stood at the nursing station, pondering how to proceed. Suddenly, an unfamiliar Asian physician arrived and asked us for the location of the patient in question. Melody suddenly threw her arms around the shorter man, gave him a vigorous snuggle, and exclaimed, "You must be Dr. Yatsuhashi! Where the fuck have you been all night?"

He looked aghast. I felt sick. I watched Dr. Yatsuhashi look at this strange nurse, momentarily stunned. Suddenly, he guffawed and answered back, "I'm right here! What do you need?" What had changed his likely planned response to her exuberant obscenity was looking at her face before answering. Once again, Melody had the kindest, most sincere, broad smile, appearing genuinely happy to see him despite that fact that moments before he had been a stranger to her. That she had, in her exultation, made a racist assumption was completely immaterial to him. In Melody's assessment, we were trying to contact a Japanese clinician who was supposed to treat our patient at Brockton Hospital. An unknown Asian man appeared unexpectedly to us on our unit, wearing scrubs. Who the fuck else would it have been but Yatsuhashi?

And then Melody got cancer. An aggressive form of cancer. Privacy was not so much an issue in the 1980s and even if it had been, we had on staff the town crier in the form of an IV nurse who traveled from floor to floor in the hospital every evening. She bore with her extraordinary skills for starting intravenous lines where others had failed. With her talent for finding veins, she left behind every bit of gossip that had come her way. For example, I was working the night John Lennon of the phenomenal band The Beatles was murdered outside the Dakota Hotel in New York by Mark David Chapman. I heard about it from Nurse Betsy before I heard it from Channel 5 News.

Likewise with Melody's sad diagnosis. Within hours after Melody's surgery, Betsy had traveled to every floor of the hospital spreading the heartbreaking information. As Betsy said, "Well, it was enough that the surgeon cried in the operating room when he realized what Melody was facing." She added, "And Melody was still under anesthesia!" Wow. In a place where bad news is the norm, news of Melody's diagnosis was like a bolt out of the blue. Everybody said, "Oh no! Not Melody."

Melody faced her diagnosis graciously. Although I left South Shore Hospital for another job a short time after hearing the bitter news, I ran into Melody often in Rexhame and at the supermarket, as we both still lived in Marshfield.

Almost always, when I saw her in town, I would just look at her, and she would answer, "Doing great!" I'd breathe a sigh of relief for Melody and her family. One day I saw her, and she simply said, "Judy, it's not so good." And yet she was at her daughter's dance recital shortly thereafter. Her daughter and my by-then three daughters all took dance classes at Roberta's School of Dance. The recitals were long and very well attended. Because the performances were recorded for posterity, people were asked to be as quiet as possible—the video camera was running. I was sitting with friends and family members enjoying my own kids' performances when Melody's daughter Anna's class completed their dance routine with remarkable flair. Melody yelled out, "*Yay, Annie! Yaaaaaaaaayyyyyyyy, Annie.*" We all recognized Melody's voice and laughed, most of us silently appreciating that Melody was still reveling in the joy of her family despite what was to come.

I have been privileged to have had Melody Monteiro in my

life. It's been many years since Melody's death from breast cancer, but each time I recall her, I do so with fondness. And I recall her raucous laughter: *"Hey, Dr. Gronberg,* look at you rolling all around the floor on your fat ass!"

In forever memory of Melody.

23

Looking Back

Yes, it is still all about Dorchester to me. I loved Dorchester, I still love Dorchester. We moved permanently out of Dorchester when I was 14 years old, although I resisted with every bone in my body. I am certain that my parents were tempted to leave their most recalcitrant child behind, but the Department of Social Services would not have allowed it.

My parents refused to let me stay in the Edwin Street home in which I insisted that I would be totally self-sufficient. I was angrily commanded to stop holding up the moving truck or else ride in it with the furniture.

I gave up the fight. I would move to Weymouth with the rest of my family, but I would return to Dorchester again and again. We left in 1968 and now, even though I am old enough to have retired from my longest full-time job, I visit Dorchester with frequency.

People always ask me, "What is it about Dorchester to you? You are obsessed." True. I belong to five different Dorchester Facebook groups, and I am often in Dorchester (usually on Route 3) on the way to spend time with my Arlington-based and Watertown-based daughters and their families. I also frequently stop at College Hype on Gallivan Boulevard for the majority of my T-shirts that are emblazoned with phrases such as "Dorchester Girl," "Originally From Dorchester," "Dorchester Triple Deckers," "OFD," or "The Parishes of Dorchester." In fact, it is commonly recognized that Dorchester is one of the only neighborhoods in the United States that is referred to not by the streets and avenues that run through it but by its Catholic parish. In my case, when people ask where I am from in Dorchester, my answer is always, "Saint Ambrose first and then Saint Mark's, but my parents were married at Saint Leo's and my father grew up in Saint Matthew's."

My favorite bakery is Greenhills in Adams Village. A popular bakery directory website describes it as follows:

Dermot Quinn has so many sweet memories of "Green-hills," his home in County Offaly, Ireland, but the fondest are of his Granny Murphy and the wonderful brown bread she would make. Since immigrating to the US, he yearned for her lovely bread. After many years of leading, Granny Murphy relented and passed this recipe and other favorite[s] on to Dermot. Her recipes are family secrets and guaranteed to please the palate. They also rekindle memories of a simpler time. Dermot and Cindy Quinn opened Greenhills Bakery, specializing in traditional and creative Irish baked goods, as a tribute to Granny Murphy (1912–1990).

I am said to be obsessed with my memories and love of Dorchester and chronicled my years until age 14 in my previous book, *Dorchester Girl*, published in 2021 by SDP Publishing.

I have said so much in both books about Dorchester, and yet in this last chapter of *Since Dorchester*, I feel that I have so much more to say. (I am often told that I am never done talking!) I will thus leave the reader with two last stories about Dorchester.

I left Dorchester 55 years ago and moved from one South Shore town to another ever farther down toward Cape Cod. In what I hope to be my last home in Duxbury, where we have resided for over 22 years, I have a painting of the Dorchester Gas Tank in my dining room, a wooden replica of Girls' Latin School (formerly in Codman Square) in my office, and a sign over the doorway to my den that says simply, "Dorchester." As I do most of my writing in my den, I display pictures of both of my grandfathers (who were Boston police officers from Dorchester), and I also have my Dorchester accent and attitude. (Those familiar with any long-term Dorchesterites will know exactly to what I am referring.)

In the 23 years in which I was teaching full-time at Curry College in Milton (a town abutting Dorchester), I had the distinct honor of teaching over 100 Boston police officers. Fortunately, or unfortunately, they encouraged my Dorchester recollections and added even more stories of their own to my repertoire.

One of the funniest of these was told to me by a Boston police officer investigating a bank robbery in Dorchester. There were numerous witnesses to the attempted robbery; one of the robbers was arrested rapidly and without incident. The robber was very forthcoming with the investigating officer, who was one of my Curry criminal justice degree students. The police officer asked him how he and his cohort thought that they would get away from the scene of the crime in a very congested area without notice. The criminal answered matter-of-factly, "We had an escape-goat outside." What he was obviously trying to convey was that they had a means of escaping with a running vehicle and a willing driver. However, he confused it with the term "scapegoat," making for a very funny story (in my humble opinion).

I will end this book with two final Dorchester stories involving the Boston Gas Tanks, located in Dorchester, and what is now referred to as the "Rainbow Gas Tank," painted by Corita Kent. I consider the Rainbow Gas Tank the ultimate symbol of Dorchester. It has a history that is meaningful to so many—those who have lived in Dorchester, those who drive through or fly over Dorchester, and those of us who own any copyrighted image of the tank that we can find.

Whenever my father drove by what started out as one gas tank when I was a child, the tank seemed to be at different heights within its cage each time that we saw it. It was. And this effect was more dramatic depending on where you were when you saw it. The tank actually floated at different levels depending on the gas pressure inside it at a given moment. Its 3-to-40-foot sections were designed to "float" in this way. I asked my Uncle Joe years later to explain to me how this worked, since he'd been employed by Boston Gas for many years. Was it an apparition or did that tank really sink sometimes?

He showed me a 1969 photo in which the expandable Boston Gas tank on the Southeast Expressway appeared to have sunk into the ground with only its red top showing. He explained that the old tank was nearly empty. The new smaller tank was able to hold much more LNG (liquefied natural gas). Construction commenced in 1969 on the second of two identical LNG tankers at Commercial Point, and "Old Fatty" was dismantled. The Boston landmark had been one of the largest gas tanks in the country, all according to Uncle Joe and supported by historical research.

The new tanks have a much more controversial story.

By 1970, a second identical LNG tank had been built beside the first. Boston now had the largest operational storage facility in the country.

The first tank was emblazoned with a rainbow swash designed in 1971 by Sister Corita Kent, an activist who demonstrated much of her social activism in her artwork.

Corita Kent (November 20, 1918–September 18, 1986, born Frances Elizabeth Kent) joined the Sisters of the Immaculate Heart religious order of Catholic nuns when she was 18. It is believed that Kent chose this order as they were known to welcome creativity and progressive ideals and activities.

Frances joined a teaching order, taking the name Sister Mary Corita. She taught for a period of time in British Columbia, but not long after returned to further her formal education. She earned her bachelor's and her master's degrees at California colleges and subsequently became head of the art department at Immaculate Heart College in Los Angeles.

Sister Corita's artwork, with its messages of love and peace, was particularly popular during the social upheavals of the 1960s and 1970s. Her political activism was prominent in her work, especially as it related to the Vietnam War and humanitarian crises. However, her work was strongly criticized, as was her college, for being too liberal. Cardinal James McIntyre labeled Corita's work blasphemous. The artist and nun returned to secular life as Corita Kent in 1968 and continued to embrace many revolutionary movements of the time. These included the anti-Vietnam War movement, the civil rights movement, and the women's rights movement. Because of continued opposition by Cardinal McIntyre to Corita, her art, and her social movement involvement, she moved to the East Coast from California to work independently.

Diagnosed with cancer in the early 1970s, Corita increased her devotion to her chosen social causes through her artwork. This fruitful time included her "Rainbow Swash" design for the LNG storage tank in Boston and the United States Postal Service's Love stamp of 1985.

In the time between her diagnosis and succumbing to her cancer, Corita Kent moved to Boston. There she confined herself to watercolor painting and printmaking. She died at age 67 in Watertown, Massachusetts. Corita Kent's legacy was her history and depiction of activism and strongly political art.

The actual painting of Dorchester's LNG tank based on Corita's design was done by Clarence Okerfelt of Okerad Signs. Okerfelt was from Weymouth, Massachusetts.

The Rainbow Swash caused controversy because it appeared to depict the profile of Ho Chi Minh in its blue paint "swash," in protest against the Vietnam War. Ho Chi Minh had been a Vietnamese revolutionary and statesman. A Marxist-Leninist, Ho Chi Minh served as President of the Democratic Republic of Vietnam, and of Vietnam, until his death in 1969. He also served as Chairman and First Secretary of the Workers' Party of Vietnam.

Corita denied that Ho Chi Minh was represented in the blue stripe of the Boston Gas Tank. After her death, when the original rainbow tank was torn down, the Rainbow Swash was recreated on the second tank in 1992 by Clarence Okerfelt's son Robert Okerfelt of Duxbury, Massachusetts. Some believe that the original blue stripe was altered slightly in its reproduction to remove any suggestion of the image of Ho Chi Minh.

Still now in 2022, the Rainbow Swash tank remains a vivid and much beloved symbol of Dorchester. It is also said to be the largest copyrighted image in the world. Those returning from flights across the world always look for the tank from the air to get that feeling of comfort that they are back in Boston. In April 2022, I returned from one of my twice-yearly trips to Ireland. As we approached Boston on our Aer Lingus flight, I quickly educated the young, male Irish citizen (cornered by me in the window seat of our row) about the significance of "the rainbow tank." He was on his first visit to the United States, and I could think of no other symbol that he would remember as well on this, his first arrival in Boston, than the sight of this historic tank.

I have to admit that our approach to our assigned runway unfortunately did not give us a peek at the tank, but I gave the Irish visitor directions to view the tank from the highway as he traversed past Commercial Point while in Boston.

Dorchester still has my heart. Right above my desk as I conclude this book is a 20- by 24-inch street map made for me by the Graphics Division of the Boston Police Department. It is entitled "Dorchester Area." Each time I drive past Tenean Beach and Malibu Beach, I gaze lovingly at the rainbow tank and open all my windows to suck in the aroma of low tide. Many things in my life have changed, and others have stayed the same . . . since Dorchester.

About the Author

Judith Kirwan Kelley was born in Dorchester, Massachusetts, in 1954 and lived there until the family joined in suburban migration, otherwise known as "white flight," in 1968. One of seven children in a typical Irish Catholic family, her relatives include, among others, Boston police officers, laborers, and housewives. Kirwan Kelley, a scholar with a Brown University PhD in sociology, considers herself a lifetime creative writer. However, Kirwan Kelley's most valuable roles are as a socially conscious, married mother of three adult daughters, and "Mimi" to her six grandchildren. Storytelling has always been part of her life.

Since Dorchester
Judith Kirwan Kelley

Publisher: SDP Publishing
Also available in ebook format

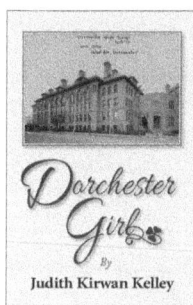

Also by the author
Judith Kirwin Kelley
Dorchester Girl

SDP Publishing

www.SDPPublishing.com
Contact us at: info@SDPPublishing.com

www.ingramcontent.com/pod-product-compliance
Lightning Source LLC
Chambersburg PA
CBHW071445090426
42737CB00011B/1784